Careers in Focus

LAW

THIRD EDITION

Ferguson

An imprint of Infobase Publishing

Careers in Focus: Law, Third Edition

Ferguson
An imprint of Infobase Publishing
132 West 31st Street
New York NY 10001

Library of Congress Cataloging-in-Publication Data

Careers in focus : law. — 3rd ed.
    p. cm.
  Includes bibliographical references and index.
  ISBN-13: 978-0-8160-7299-6 (alk. paper)
  ISBN-10: 0-8160-7299-X (alk. paper)
  1. Law—Vocational guidance—United States—Juvenile literature. 2. Law—Vocational guidance. 3. Vocational guidance. I. Ferguson Publishing.
  KF297.C37 2009
  340.023'73—dc22
                              2008036453

Ferguson books are available at special discounts when purchased in bulk quantities for businesses, associations, institutions, or sales promotions. Please call our Special Sales Department in New York at (212) 967-8800 or (800) 322-8755.

You can find Ferguson on the World Wide Web at http://www.fergpubco.com

Text design by David Strelecky
Cover design by Salvatore Luongo

Printed in the United States of America

Sheriden MSRF 10 9 8 7 6 5 4 3 2 1

This book is printed on acid-free paper.

Table of Contents

Introduction

Since the dawn of civilization, man has depended on law and order. One cannot exist without the other. Without laws, nobody would know the boundaries of appropriate behavior, and civilization would seem a lot less civilized. Without order, people could not be held responsible for their actions. For this reason, the field of law includes a diverse spectrum of career opportunities that are as demanding as they are in demand in today's society.

Almost every community has its own police department. A police force may have specialized divisions, such as narcotics squad to combat illegal drugs; a vice squad to fight rape, prostitution, and related crimes; a SWAT team that can be called upon in emergency situations; a hostage rescue team; and a bomb squad. Patrol officers may become detectives. *Police officers* may rise through the ranks to become sergeants, lieutenants, or even the chief of police for a community. Many other people provide support for a police department, from traffic clerks and police clerks to forensic experts and polygraph examiners.

Other important areas of local law enforcement are probation and parole services. *Probation officers* are generally attached to the court system, while *parole officers* work with the correctional system. Both work in cooperation with the police department.

The incarceration and rehabilitation of suspected and convicted criminals also occurs at each of the local, state, and federal levels. Communities usually operate jails, which provide temporary sentencing to permanent prisons. The prison system operates minimum, medium, and maximum security prisons, depending on the nature of the criminal and the crime. Special prisons house mentally ill prisoners or juvenile offenders. People convicted of federal crimes are generally sent to prisons operated by the federal government.

The U.S. Marshals Service, part of the U.S. Department of Justice, is concerned with crimes that cross state lines. Interstate crimes, as they are called, may involve the transport of stolen vehicles and goods from one state to another. *U.S. marshals* are responsible for tracking down wanted criminals and transporting prisoners. They also operate the Federal Witness Security Program and provide security for federal courts and judges.

The other half of the law field is devoted to the prosecution and defense of those accused of breaking the law. The main players in the legal profession in the United States are lawyers and judges, whose basic tasks are to interpret and apply the law. Basically, *lawyers* explain the law to their clients and advise them concerning the status of their cases. Supporting lawyers are paralegals and legal secretaries. *Paralegals* and *legal secretaries* assist lawyers by doing some of the vital "grunt" work that needs to be accomplished, such as interviewing witnesses, conducting research, and examining documents.

Lawyers have opportunities to practice law in a variety of areas. Most lawyers base this choice on what subject they are interested in, the people they want to work with, and where they want to live while doing that work. The possibilities include working for a private company, a government agency, a corporate law firm, or a public interest law firm. In addition, lawyers may serve as judges or become instructors and professors in colleges or universities.

Judges preside over court proceedings and make judgments concerning how laws are to be applied in our judicial system. On the federal level, the judicial system is made up of a series of courts. The Supreme Court is the highest court of the land and rules on issues related to the U.S. Constitution. The Supreme Court is made up of nine justices, appointed by the president with consent of the Senate, who review selected decisions made at the state level. The Circuit Court of Appeals deals with decisions that have been appealed by the district courts and reviews judgments of lower courts. The District Courts are the third level of the federal court system, servicing approximately 100 zones, or districts, across the country. Each state also has its own judicial system that is separate from the federal system. Most civil and criminal cases are tried in state courts. These cases can move on to a federal court if they are related to an issue concerning the Constitution. Most cities also have municipal courts to handle minor cases.

No matter what level the court, many individuals besides the judge and the attorneys are needed to make it run smoothly. Before court is even in session, a *bail bondsman* plays a role. Bail bondsmen pay the bail to allow someone who has been arrested and is awaiting trial to go free for the time being. In exchange, the person who was arrested agrees to pay the bondsman a certain percentage of the bond assigned by the court. *Process servers* are licensed by the courts to serve legal papers to the people or corporations that are involved in legal disputes. Inside the courtroom, *bailiffs* are court officers that keep the peace of the court, make sure witnesses are ushered in and out of the courtroom, hand evidence directly to the witnesses, and maintain order. *Court reporters document the events in court for the official record by transcribing the words* and actions of the judge, attorneys, and witnesses.

Careers in protective services are projected to grow about as fast as the average for all occupations through 2016, as are most jobs within public service, according to the U.S. Department of Labor. Increases in crime rates, and especially increases in public anxiety over crime, have led to demands for heightened law enforcement efforts, tougher sentencing laws, and dramatic increases in the security services industry.

According to the Bureau of Justice Statistics, 7.6 million Americans were on probation, in jail or prison, or on parole at the end of 2006—1 in every 31 U.S. adults or 3.2 percent of the population. Nearly 1.6 million were in state or federal prison in mid-2007. The war on drugs has had an especially great impact on the numbers of people being sent to prison. Public outrage at the early release of many violent criminals has led to demands for legislation ensuring these criminals serve the full length of their sentences. More prisons are being built to accommodate them, and more corrections officers are being hired to guard them. At the same time, the overcrowding of many correctional facilities has stimulated pressure for more liberal probation and parole efforts, requiring greater numbers of parole and probation officers.

Lawyers and other legal personnel will be needed to focus on modern concerns, such as employee benefits, consumer protection, estates and trusts, and the environment. However, there will be stiff competition for jobs involving the law through 2016. Lawyers who want to become judges will face even stiffer competition.

In response to this changing demand, law school graduates are increasingly looking outside the conventional law fields for a career. Organizations such as banks, real estate firms, insurance companies, and government agencies consider knowledge of law an asset, if not a requirement, for a job.

However, the need for law professionals will remain a constant as business interactions increase and gain complexity and law counsel is needed in areas such as medicine, intellectual property, corporate harassment, and the environment.

Each article in this book discusses a particular law occupation in detail. Many of the articles in *Careers in Focus: Law* appear in Ferguson's *Encyclopedia of Careers and Vocational Guidance* but have been updated and revised with the latest information from the U.S. Department of Labor and other sources. The **Overview** section is a brief introductory description of the duties and responsibilities of someone in this career. Oftentimes, a career may have a variety of job titles. When this is the case, alternative career titles are presented in this section. The **History** section describes the history of the particular job as it relates to the overall development of its industry or field. **The Job** describes the primary and secondary duties of the job. **Requirements** discusses high school and postsecondary education and training requirements for success in the job. **Exploring** offers suggestions on how to gain some experience in or knowledge of the particular job before making a firm educational and financial commitment. The focus is on what can be done while still in high school (or in the early years of college) to gain a better understanding of the job. The **Employers** section gives an overview of typical places of employment for the job. **Starting Out** discusses the best ways to land that first job, be it through the college placement office, newspaper ads, or personal contact. The **Advancement** section describes what kind of career path to expect from the job and how to get there. **Earnings** lists salary ranges and describes the typical fringe benefits. The **Work Environment** section describes the typical surroundings and conditions of employment—whether indoors or outdoors, noisy or quiet, social or independent, and so on. Also discussed are typical hours worked, any seasonal fluctuations, and the stresses and strains of the job. The **Outlook** section summarizes the job in terms of the general economy and industry projections. For the most part, Outlook information is obtained from the Bureau of Labor Statistics and is supplemented by information taken from professional associations. Job growth terms follow those used in the *Occupational Outlook Handbook*. Growth described as "much faster than the average" means an increase of 21 percent or more. Growth described as "faster than the average" means an increase of 14 to 20 percent. Growth described as "about as fast as the average" means an increase of 7 to 13 percent. Growth described as "more slowly than the average" means an increase of 3 to 6 percent. "Little or no change" means a decrease of 2 percent to an increase of 2 percent. "Decline" means a decrease of 3 percent or more. Each article ends with **For More Information**, which lists organizations that can provide career information on training, education, internships, scholarships, and job placement.

Careers in Focus: Law also includes photographs, informative sidebars, and interviews with professionals in the field.

Bail Bondsmen

OVERVIEW

When someone is arrested for a crime, a *bail bondsman* (also known as a *bail agent* or *bail bonding agent*) pays the bail so that person can go free until it is time for the trial. The bondsman charges a fee of 10 to 15 percent of the total cash bond assigned by the court. If the person doesn't appear for trial, the bondsman must either find the person or hire someone, known as a *bail enforcement agent, fugitive recovery agent,* or *bounty hunter,* to find the person and bring him or her back. Because the work bondsmen do relies on criminal activities, larger cities have the greatest need for bondsmen. There are approximately 14,500 bail bondsmen employed in the United States.

HISTORY

Bail bonding is a long-established tradition of the American legal system. Posting bail to temporarily free someone who is accused of a crime began in colonial times. Colonists lived under English common law, wherein people who were charged with crimes were released if someone in the community would vouch for them. At first, if the accused person didn't show up for the trial, the person who guaranteed the accused person's appearance had to face the punishment that would have been given to the accused person. Later, this practice changed so that property was used to guarantee the appearance of someone for trial. In that way, if the person failed to appear for trial, the person who promised that the accused would appear only lost property and did not have to face punishment. As crime increased and the need for making sure accused people showed up for court grew, the

QUICK FACTS

School Subjects
Business
Government
Mathematics

Personal Skills
Communication/ideas
Leadership/management

Work Environment
Indoors and outdoors
Primarily multiple locations

Minimum Education Level
Some postsecondary training

Salary Range
$24,600 to $43,870 to
$115,090+

Certification or Licensing
Required by certain states

Outlook
About as fast as the average

DOT
186

GOE
04.03.01

NOC
N/A

O*NET-SOC
N/A

courts continued to allow the practice of posting bail. In fact, the Eighth Amendment to the U.S. Constitution states: "Excessive bail shall not be required, nor excessive fines imposed, nor cruel and unusual punishments inflicted." Bail bonding today allows jail space to be freed for serious criminals and helps to ensure that everyone is truly innocent until proven guilty.

THE JOB

Bail bondsmen work to ensure that a person released from jail will appear again in court as ordered. A typical case a bail bondsman handles may play out like this: It's late at night and the bondsman's office phone rings. A woman on the other end of the line says her son has been arrested and his court date for trial is four months down the road. The judge set her son's bail at $30,000, and she doesn't have that kind of money. She doesn't want her son to sit in jail for four months for something she's sure he didn't do. The mother wants the bondsman's help in getting her son out on bail. She offers to pay the bondsman's fee, which at 10 percent of the bail amount would be $3,000, in exchange for the bondsman covering the bail. Although the bondsman may have doubts about the arrested person's guilt or innocence, that's not an issue for the bondsman to decide. What the bondsman does have to decide is whether or not the person is a good risk—if he doesn't show up for his court date, the bondsman loses the money posted for bail. Before deciding to take the case, the bondsman does research. Using the phone and computers, the bonding agent gathers more information, such as the type of crime the son allegedly committed, any past record he may have, if he works and what his employer says about him, and what ties he has to the community. After this research, the bondsman may decide to post bond or reject the case. If the bondsman takes the case and posts bond, and the client shows up for his court date, the bondsman gets the posted money back. If the client fails to show up for court, either the bondsman himself goes after the client or the bondsman hires bounty hunters (also known as bail enforcement agents and fugitive recovery agents) to track down the son and bring him back. Depending on the state, the court gives the bondsman from 90 to 180 days to have the defendant back for trial before bail money is forfeited to the court system.

Like insurance agents, bail bondsmen are calculated risk takers. Every time they decide to post bail for someone, they are taking a financial risk. Most bondsmen have reliability standards that they use to determine whether someone is more likely to show up for court or to run and hide. The bondsman looks into the person's criminal record, employment history, living arrangements, family situation, and community ties. The type of alleged crime also affects whether a person will run. A bondsman also looks into the arrestee's past criminal record and the state's case against him or her. People who have a history of crime patterns, such as prostitutes and drug users, are considered bad risks. On the other hand, drug dealers and professional criminals are good risks because these groups of people usually need to stay in the same area, and they want to keep the trust of a bondsman so they can rely on him or her later.

To help cut down the risk of someone "jumping bail," the bondsman spends a lot of time monitoring the people for whom bail has been posted. Some even include a stipulation in the agreement for posting bail that the accused person must call in on a regular basis to verify his or her whereabouts. If the accused person isn't calling in on schedule, the bondsman can get a head start on tracking down the client.

For some bondsmen, tracking down bail jumpers is part of their job, and it takes up much of their time. Other bondsmen choose to hire bounty hunters, who capture and return the client to the bondsman for a fee. Sometimes the bondsman will pay the bounty hunter as much as 50 percent of the total bond if the accused person is returned. The bondsman pays this high amount because it's better to lose half the money that has been posted for bail than to lose all the money if the runaway isn't returned. For the bail bondsman who takes tracking into his or her own hands, the search can lead all over the country. The bondsmen call the accused's family, friends, employers, and anyone they can find to try and get a lead that will eventually take them to the bail jumper. They use computer databases to check into records showing credit activity, estates, and death certificates. When the person is located, the bondsman or bounty hunter confronts the individual and brings him or her back. For a potentially dangerous "skip," the bounty hunter and a backup team may have to break down a door with guns drawn, or opt to work with the local sheriff's department in the instance of known violent offenders.

Some bondsmen use firearms to protect themselves from possible harm. However, the bail bondsman's job is mostly desk work, and often the reason a client misses a court date is because he or she has overslept, forgotten about it, or thought it was for a different day and time.

REQUIREMENTS

While the qualifications vary from state to state, the basic requirements for a bail bondsman are to be at least 18 or 21 years of age, have a high school diploma or GED, and have no felony police record.

High School

To prepare for a career as a bail bondsman, focus on computers, accounting, mathematics, government, social studies, and geography. Accounting, computers, and mathematics will prepare you to handle bookkeeping, record keeping, and negotiations concerning bail money. Because you'll be using a computer to trace bail jumpers, try to spend as much time as you can honing your computer skills.

Postsecondary Training

Some college-level course work in criminal justice and psychology and training in law enforcement techniques are helpful for this career. Many of today's bail bondsmen have college degrees in criminal justice, although that is not a requirement. Depending on your state's regulations, you may need to complete a certain amount of specific pre-work and pre-licensing education. For example, one of Oklahoma's requirements for those wishing to work as bail bondsmen is to complete 16 hours of education sponsored by the Oklahoma Bondsman Association before they can sit for their licensing exam and begin working.

Certification or Licensing

Some states require would-be bail bondsmen to attain a property and casualty insurance license requiring several hours of class work under the jurisdiction of the State Director of Insurance or State Department of Professional Regulation. Wisconsin, Illinois, Oregon, and Kentucky ban for-profit bail bonding altogether. Other states require you to pass a bail-bond certification exam. Most states that require exams or licensing also require several hours of continuing education classes each year to keep the license current. You will need a gun license if you plan to use a firearm.

Other Requirements

Bail bondsmen need to have people skills that allow them to effectively communicate with the clients and law enforcement officers they contact daily. They must also be able to deal with high levels of stress and tense situations. Bail bondsmen who do not hire bounty hunters must be physically fit in order to be prepared for any violent or challenging situation.

EXPLORING

You can explore this career by becoming familiar with the justice system. For example, ask your high school guidance counselor or government teacher to help you arrange a visit to the local police department. You can get a tour of the facilities, learn about arrest procedures, and hear from law enforcement professionals. In some cases, you may be able to arrange for a police ride-along to get a taste of what it takes to arrest or confront someone who does not want to cooperate. You can also familiarize yourself with the justice system by sitting in on open court proceedings. Another option is to give a bail bondsman a call and ask questions. Search "bail bonding" on the Internet to see just how many bail bondsmen are out there; check out their Web sites to learn what kinds of services are offered. Finally, try to get a part-time job that allows you to deal face-to-face with other people—anything from a crowd-control team member at a concert to a security assistant at an amusement park. Working for a security office or for the local court system as a background checker is great experience as well.

EMPLOYERS

Approximately 14,500 bail bondsmen are employed in the United States. Bail bondsmen usually work for other bondsmen or own their own small businesses. Many bondsmen join together to form a partnership to share the workload and to pool their resources. Established bondsmen usually hire several young bondsmen to do the background checking and research. Although almost all towns and cities have bail bondsmen at work, most bondsmen are in large towns and cities. The larger the population, the greater the opportunity for crime and the greater the number of crimes committed, which means the greater the need for bail bonds to be posted.

STARTING OUT

You probably won't see as many ads in the newspaper for bondsmen as you do for other careers, but keep an eye on the classifieds anyway—especially in the big city newspapers. If you want a more direct approach, try calling your local police for some recommendations of experienced bondsmen that you can contact to inquire about a job. Before becoming a bondsman, get your feet wet by doing background checks, chasing down leads, and handling paperwork. If work as a bondsman isn't immediately available, start out in related jobs, such as security positions. Quite a number of bail agents also start out in the insurance business, learning such things as risk assessment and how to underwrite bonds.

ADVANCEMENT

A bail bondsman can remain an independent agent, owning his or her own business, or can advance to managerial positions with a managing general agent. In a partnership, a bondsman can advance to become the *supervising bondsman,* assigning work to more inexperienced bondsmen. There are various jobs that relate to the work of bail bondsmen, such as *property and casualty insurance agent, detective,* and the court system jobs of *pretrial release officer, release on recognizance worker,* and *probation officer.*

EARNINGS

Because most bondsmen have their own businesses, earnings vary according to how much time and effort is invested in the job. Another important factor influencing the earnings of bail bondsmen is the number of their clients who show up for their court dates. According to the National Center for Policy Analysis in Dallas, Texas, 95 percent of a bondsman's clients must show up in court for the business to be successful. According to information from the *Occupational Outlook Quarterly,* a Bureau of Labor Statistics publication, bail bondsmen just starting out and working for a firm may have yearly earnings of approximately $25,000. The bails set for many common charges, such as driving under the influence (DUI) and drug possession, are often not extremely high, perhaps ranging from $500 or $600 to $3,000 or $4,000. In these cases a bondsman would earn $50 or $60 to $300 or $400; because of these low amounts a bondsman must successfully handle quite a few cases a year to make a substantial living. While a specific annual salary range is difficult to determine, it may be helpful to consider earnings for insurance sales agents since bondsmen's work is similar to that of insurance agents and they are often regulated under state departments of insurance. According to the U.S. Department of Labor, the median yearly income for insurance sales agents in 2006 was $43,870. Fifty percent earned between $31,640 and $69,180 that same year, while the lowest 10 percent had earnings of $24,600 or less, and the highest 10 percent had earnings of $115,090 or more. Earnings also depend on where the bondsman conducts business. Larger cities offer the most opportunity to make money; however, a well-run business in a medium-sized city can also be highly profitable.

Bondsmen working for firms may receive typical benefits such as health insurance and vacation time. Those who run their own businesses must pay for such benefits themselves.

WORK ENVIRONMENT

Bondsmen work in offices; some do the work from their homes. Usually the bondsman is located close to the courthouse so the accused can get immediate service. Bondsmen can work alone or as a team with other bondsmen and people who monitor clients and research background information. Bondsmen spend a lot of time doing paperwork; they must keep records detailing all of their actions and contracts with clients.

Bail bondsmen who choose to do their own tracking may also spend time traveling to find bail jumpers. Tracking bail jumpers and bringing them back to court can be dangerous because these people are obviously desperate to remain free.

Bail bonding is not a nine-to-five job. Because people get arrested at all hours, and bondsmen are on call 24 hours a day. If a bail jumper needs to be rounded up, hours are spent in surveillance to determine just the right moment to move in.

Bondsmen are in contact with many different people during the course of a day. They interview friends and relatives of a bail jumper and work with court personnel. Bondsmen use beepers and cellular phones to remain available to clients who may need their services.

OUTLOOK

Opportunities for bail-bonding work are growing as people with criminal justice, law enforcement, and insurance training enter and gain success in the field, thus gaining the public's respect for the necessity of this work. The Bail Bond Fairness Act of 2007 has also improved employment opportunities for bail bondsmen; it makes it easier for bail bondsmen to work with defendants who have been charged at the federal level. Professional Bail Agents of the United States says the bail bondsman career is a growing field, but the use of personal recognizance bail has had a negative impact on its growth. (When judges release an accused person on their own personal recognizance, there is no need for bail bond service; however, there is also no guarantee that the person will show up for court.)

Bail bonding is an industry under constant scrutiny by the justice system, primarily because of the authority of the bail bondsman to engage in activities that some law enforcers cannot perform (such as entering homes without a warrant) and what is said to be a financial rather than moral interest in bringing criminals back to trial.

FOR MORE INFORMATION

Visit the coalition's Web site for information on bail laws and bounty hunter laws nationwide, state associations, and industry news.

American Bail Coalition
1725 Desales Street, NW, Suite 800
Washington, DC 20036-4410

Tel: 800-375-8390
Email: dnabic@aol.com
http://www.americanbailcoalition.com

For general information about the field and for specific information about working in California, contact
California Bail Agents Association
One Capitol Mall, Suite 320
Sacramento, CA 95814-3228
Tel: 916-446-3038
http://www.cbaa.com

For more information on the work of bail bondsmen and links of interest, visit the PBUS Web site.
Professional Bail Agents of the United States (PBUS)
1301 Pennsylvania Avenue, NW, Suite 925
Washington, DC 20004-1719
Tel: 202-783-4120
Email: info@pbus.com
http://www.pbus.com

Bailiffs

OVERVIEW

From keeping the courtroom secure to providing food and housing for sequestered juries, the *bailiff* is responsible for managing the court's business. Bailiffs also serve legal papers to individuals and businesses as ordered by the court. Although the majority of bailiffs work for the court system, some bailiffs are more like process servers because they work independently and own their own businesses. There are approximately 18,000 bailiffs employed in the United States.

HISTORY

The first bailiffs date back to medieval England. Bailiffs in this time period were either in charge of managing a manor or managing a court. Bailiffs who worked for manors or estates had the responsibility of collecting fines and rent as well as supervising the activities on the grounds. Court bailiffs helped the judges during the two sessions of the Royal Court that were held every year. The early predecessor of the modern bailiff had police authority to protect the court and serve legal papers as well.

In America, the constable performed many of the duties that now fall on the bailiff's shoulders. Along with the more pressing duty of keeping the peace, the constable attended to the courts and was responsible for taking care of jury members.

Today, a bailiff is considered an officer of the court who has the authority to serve legal papers and confiscate property. Like the medieval bailiff and the American constable, modern bailiffs are responsible for attending to the needs of the court while it is in session and out of session.

THE JOB

The majority of bailiffs in the United States serve in the court or legal system; however, some bailiffs own their own service businesses. Most people are more familiar with the *courtroom bailiff* who instructs people in the court to rise and be seated when the judge does and who swears in witnesses. These tasks and many others make up the courtroom bailiff's main duty, which is to serve the judge and the courtroom to which he or she is assigned. Depending on the state in which the bailiff is employed and the judge, the duties vary, but all bailiffs in the court system have some common responsibilities. First, the bailiff must maintain order during trials. Security is an important part of the bailiff's job. Although the judge and the jury are the bailiff's first concern, every person in the courtroom is under the care of the bailiff as far as personal safety is concerned. If a bailiff is in tune with the goings-on in the court, potential problems can be avoided and trouble can be spotted before it erupts. Bailiffs are most respected if they run a safe and secure courtroom.

For Armando Suarez, a security transportation officer for the Juvenile Court in Allen County, Indiana, ensuring secure transportation and a safe environment at court are large parts of his job. "My primary responsibility is the transfer of juvenile inmates between the detention facility and our local courthouse. Once at the courthouse, my partner and I are responsible for maintaining security and safety in the juvenile courts division."

The bailiff is basically the judge's right hand. The bailiff swears in witnesses, handles articles of evidence, escorts prisoners to and from court, prepares reports, and does whatever else the judge may ask. Paperwork is also a segment of the bailiff's responsibilities, although the focus depends on the type of court in which the bailiff serves. "I am also responsible for processing all juvenile warrants by dispersing them to local law enforcement and issuing notices of cancellation when appropriate," Suarez says. "Another part of my job entails collecting criminal records on those whom the court has ordered such information collected. This can be either on parents or guardians of juveniles in custody, persons applying for positions in the juvenile courts, or for purposes of determining court dispositions." Bailiffs must also remind people of courtroom rules and enforce those rules if necessary. For example, a bailiff may tell someone in the court that smoking is not allowed or that their conversation is interrupting court proceedings. If necessary, the bailiff may remove uncooperative persons from the courtroom.

Courtroom bailiffs are often also charged with taking care of the jury. When juries are sequestered, that is, not allowed to return to their homes during a trial, the bailiff must make arrangements for their food and lodging during the entire trial process. The bailiff usually accompanies jury members to any public places, such as restaurants, to make sure they do not have contact with the public. If a bailiff fails to keep the jury from seeing or hearing anything about the case at hand, the jury members may have to be replaced and the court proceedings brought to a grinding halt. The bailiff also serves as a guard wherever the jury is staying.

Outside the confines of the courtroom and the responsibilities of the jury, the bailiff also serves legal papers such as court summonses, restraining orders, and jury summonses. *Independent bailiffs* also serve this function. They act as process servers and track down individuals or companies to serve them legal documents. Independent bailiffs also collect money or property that has defaulted back under a lease, lien, or mortgage. A bailiff may get an assignment to repossess a vehicle, for instance, or to inform tenants that the landlord is throwing them out because they haven't paid the rent for six months. Independent bailiff work is usually done on an assignment or contract basis in which someone calls the bailiff and pays for a specific, one-time service.

REQUIREMENTS
High School
Do you find the idea of managing a courtroom intriguing? If you think a career as a bailiff might be right for you, start preparing for it while you're still in school. Take political science, communications, and law-related high school courses. If you have the opportunity to earn certificates in emergency skills, such as CPR or triage, take advantage of it as you prepare for a career that is centered on security and safety. Jim Marlow of Niagara Bailiff Services recommends computers and communication classes. "I believe this industry will rely more and more on technology in the future. Also, since this business has a lot of interaction between people, and sometimes these people are not happy to see us, I would recommend any course that would sharpen your 'people' skills."

Postsecondary Training
Many states require bailiffs to have training from police academies or from other programs approved by the local government's law enforcement training board. Smaller cities may substitute on-the-job training for police academy training. Since many courtroom bailiffs are assigned by sheriff's offices, the education requirements for bailiffs are generally the same as for other law enforcement officers. In fact, a

good course of action is to contact your local sheriff's department and find out what deputy sheriff training programs are available. When you have completed the program and secured a position in the sheriff's department, you will have an inside edge for moving into a bailiff job. Training usually involves class work, meeting physical requirements, and getting supervised hands-on experience. Although college education is usually not required, many junior or community colleges offer classes related to public safety or protective services careers. Courses such as criminal law, report writing and communications, police functions, and ethics in the justice system can help you learn the courts and this type of work. The International Association of Court Officers & Services (IACO&S), an affiliate of the National Sheriffs' Association (NSA), offers training, workshops, and seminars covering topics such as court security, transportation, and legal issues. IACO&S and NSA also sponsor a yearly court security conference. The NSA Web site (http://www.sheriffs.org) has more information on training and the IACO&S.

Certification or Licensing

Although most states do not require specific bailiff certification, certification as a peace officer or officer of the court is often required. States vary in their requirements; for example, requirements for bailiff certification in Missouri include completing a Peace Officer Standards and Training program, being at least 21 years of age, being a U.S. citizen, and having no criminal history. Candidates who fulfill such requirements and pass the Missouri Peace Officer Certification exam are then certified peace officers and can work as bailiffs. Other states may require bailiffs to be licensed law enforcement officers, such as police officers or sheriff's deputies. Some employers, such as sheriff's departments, may require bailiffs to have firearms certification. Other employers may require bailiffs to have valid driver's licenses for the state in which they work. Check with the law enforcement agency or your local courthouse to find out the specific requirements for your state.

Other Requirements

Bailiffs interact with many different kinds of people. From the judge, to the inmate, to the jury member, the bailiff must communicate effectively to ensure the organized flow of information in the courtroom. Bailiffs must be good listeners as well, because they must respond to requests for information and react to disturbances and problems. To be a successful bailiff, you must be able to speak clearly, respond quickly, concentrate on the task at hand, and be aware of potential trouble.

A bailiff escorts a defendant to a court arraignment. *(The Paducah Sun, Barkley Thieleman, AP Images)*

Also, because most bailiffs must be trained as law enforcement officers, you will need to pass physically demanding tests. Drug tests are also part of the requirements for becoming a peace officer.

EXPLORING

Do you like the sound of a career as a bailiff? If you'd like to know what it would really be like, take some steps on your own to explore the career and get some inside information. Any contact you can have with law enforcement officers will be a big plus. Contact your local police station and request a tour of the facilities. Explain that you are considering a law enforcement career and ask if anyone would be willing to talk to you about typical police work. Sit in on some hearings or trials at your local courthouse and pay close attention to every move the bailiff makes. Try to spot his or her main duties. Try to arrange an interview either at the courthouse or over the phone to ask the questions you'll no doubt have after seeing the bailiff in action. Talk to your guidance counselor or political science teacher about arranging a "Students in Court" day in which you and your friends play the role of different officers of the court in a mock trial. Do some research and interview a bailiff or two before the mock trial. Check into volunteer programs; many courts allow high school students to volunteer in various ways. If a program doesn't exist, suggest creating one to your school counselor or principal.

EMPLOYERS

Approximately 18,000 bailiffs are employed in the United States. Most bailiffs work for the state and local courts and are employed by sheriff departments. Some bailiffs are assigned to actual courtrooms and others are assigned to specific judges. Bailiffs work throughout the country, but more bailiff positions are usually found in larger cities as compared to the smaller ones. Independent bailiffs also work all across the country, although they too usually find more work in larger cities.

STARTING OUT

To get into the bailiff field, you must either be appointed by the sheriff's office or be hired after gaining experience as a peace officer. According to Armando Suarez, employment in the sheriff's office is the most common way to become a bailiff: "Most bailiffs are usually sheriffs' deputies or court officers assigned to work in the courts by the sheriff. If you are interested in this line of work, a career in law enforcement, specifically on a sheriff's department, would be the way to go." After you are working in the sheriff's department, making your desire to be a bailiff known is the best way to get an opportunity to move into that position when it becomes available.

ADVANCEMENT

Bailiffs can advance to many careers in the area of law enforcement. Because most bailiffs are appointed by the sheriff's office, they remain under the supervision of the sheriff. Bailiffs can often move into supervisory roles within the sheriff's department when they are prepared to end their work as bailiffs. Bailiffs can move laterally and become deputies focusing on something other than court security, or they can move up to become second-in-command or even sheriff. Additional training and experience are needed to move up to higher positions. Other possibilities include correctional officer and supervisory police officer. The many duties that a bailiff performs are an excellent preparation for most all other positions in law enforcement.

EARNINGS

Earnings for bailiffs are often subject to the budget amounts in the sheriff's department where the bailiff works. Bailiffs working for large, well-funded departments will have higher earnings than those at small departments with limited budgets. The U.S. Department of Labor (USDL) reports that bailiffs had a median yearly income of $34,210 in 2006. In addition, the USDL estimates 10 percent of bailiffs earned less than $18,390 annually and 10 percent earned more than $58,270 a year in 2006. Bailiffs employed in local government had mean annual earnings of $32,400 in 2006, while those working for state governments earned $47,370.

Independent bailiffs are usually paid on a per-service contract, so income varies according to the prices set by the independent bailiff. Jim Marlow adds, "It is difficult to peg a salary for bailiffs, as most operate their own business. Bailiffs that work for another bailiff are usually paid a commission on the work completed."

Bailiffs usually receive comparable benefits to other sheriff's officers and deputies. Insurance, pension, vacation days, and other benefits are set by individual sheriff's departments.

WORK ENVIRONMENT

Most of a bailiff's workday is spent indoors in a courtroom or in an office building. The bailiff works with many different people, including all the courtroom personnel, not to mention other law enforcement officials, probation officers, court clerks, and so on. A bailiff is seldom alone and must interact with others all day long. Because of the nature of the work, bailiffs are often placed in stressful situations and sometimes even dangerous ones. When not in the courtroom, a bailiff may transport prisoners or jury members to and from the courthouse. Bailiffs are also called on to leave the courtroom to serve papers or to conduct other official court business. Most of the bailiff's 40- to 45-hour workweek is spent inside the courtroom; the remaining hours are spent serving papers and performing other miscellaneous duties.

OUTLOOK

The bailiff career is a long-established one, and bailiffs are considered indispensable in courtroom settings. Because of this, bailiffs are needed and will continue to be a major part of the courtroom system. However, competition for positions in the entire law enforcement field is keen due to such factors as the challenges these jobs offer and the sense of purpose these job provide. In addition, the number of positions available may also be affected by local government funding.

Job opportunities should be best in urban areas with lowering paying positions and relatively high crime rates. Other job openings will result from turnover as officers retire, transfer to other positions, or leave the field. Because the number of positions available depends on the amount of turnover and budgetary constraints, the number of job opportunities varies from year to year and from place to place.

FOR MORE INFORMATION

The American Bar Association's Division for Public Education provides information to teachers, students, and the general public about law education projects at the state and national level, careers in law, a glossary of legal terms, and more on its Web site.

American Bar Association
Division for Public Education
321 North Clark Street
Chicago, IL 60610-4714
Tel: 800-285-2221
http://www.abanet.org/publiced

For more information on training opportunities and conferences, contact

National Sheriffs' Association
1450 Duke Street
Alexandria, VA 22314-3490
Tel: 800-424-7827
http://www.sheriffs.org

You will need to contact your local law enforcement office or state's commission on peace officer training to find out about opportunities in your area. However, to get a general idea of what this training involves, visit the informative California Commission on Peace Officer Standards and Training Web site.

California Commission on Peace Officer Standards and Training
http://www.post.ca.gov

Bank Examiners

OVERVIEW

Bank examiners investigate financial institutions to ensure their safety and soundness and to enforce federal and state laws. They arrange audits, review policies and procedures, study documents, and interview managers and employees. They prepare detailed reports that can be used to strengthen banks.

A bank examiner's fundamental duty is to make sure people do not lose the money they have entrusted to banks. Bank examiners protect account holders. They also protect the federal and state governments that are responsible for insuring financial institutions. There are approximately 26,000 financial examiners employed In the United States.

HISTORY

The First Bank of the United States, founded in Philadelphia in 1791, was an unqualified success. It acted as the federal government's banker and received private and business deposits. The bank issued banknotes that could be exchanged for gold and succeeded in creating a national currency. In 1811, the visionary experiment came to an untimely end; despite the bank's many successes, its charter was not renewed. In a time when states' rights were considered supreme, a national bank was an unpopular idea.

The second national bank fared just as well—but no better. Despite an impressive list of achievements, the bank failed when President Andrew Jackson vetoed its charter renewal.

For the next several decades, the nation adhered to a system of "free banking," meaning that bank charters were readily granted to groups that met limited standards. The number of state banks

QUICK FACTS

School Subjects
English
Mathematics

Personal Skills
Communication/ideas
Leadership/management

Work Environment
Primarily indoors
One location with some
  travel

Minimum Education Level
Bachelor's degree

Salary Range
$34,790 to $65,370 to
  $118,000+

Certification or Licensing
Required

Outlook
About as fast as the average

DOT
160

GOE
13.02.04

NOC
N/A

O*NET-SOC
13-2061.00

multiplied rapidly. Each state bank issued its own banknotes, creating an untenable currency system.

In the 1860s, the U.S. Civil War destroyed the South's economy. Banks in the southern states did not have the resources to weather the difficulties. The only national financial organization, the Independent Treasury, was ill-equipped to meet the ensuing financial demands. The price of "free banking" became painfully clear.

In 1864, as the nation struggled to rebuild itself, the federal government passed the National Bank Act. Intended to bring about economic stability and prevent future bank failures, the act created the Office of the Comptroller of the Currency (OCC). The OCC initially had the power to charter national banks that could issue national banknotes. The OCC also was the first organization to conduct bank examinations.

Unfortunately, the National Bank Act of 1864 did not bring about the desired stability. Over the next several decades, the country experienced four bank panics, the worst of which occurred in 1907. Bank panics were characterized by "runs on the banks," during which people became fearful and tried to withdraw all of their money at once. The banks often did not have enough cash in reserve and many failed. The Federal Reserve Act (1913) created a centralized reserve system that could lend banks money and prevent bank crises.

In its early form, the Federal Reserve System was unable to prevent the bank failures that led, in 1929, to the Great Depression. In 1933, in response to the Depression, the Federal Reserve's powers were extended. The Federal Reserve eventually would become a central bank that actively promoted monetary stability. Like the OCC, the Federal Reserve now regularly examines banks.

The Federal Deposit Insurance Corporation (FDIC) also was created in 1933. The FDIC pays depositors if an insured bank closes without the resources to repay people their money. The FDIC also is charged with the responsibility of preventing unsound banking practices within the banks it insures. The FDIC regularly examines all the banks it insures in order to ensure their safety and soundness. Since its creation, the FDIC has successfully prevented any widespread bank panics.

The years since 1933 have not been without challenges, however. In the mid-1980s, hundreds of savings and loan banks failed, reinforcing the need for the regular, thorough examination of banks by the OCC, the Federal Reserve, the FDIC, and a number of other federal and state agencies. Today, most banks are examined on an annual basis, often by more than one regulatory organization.

THE JOB

When many people think of bank examiners, they envision the examiner from *It's a Wonderful Life*—a humorless bureaucrat who threatens to destroy George Bailey. In reality, bank examiners are public servants. They work to ensure that our nation's banks remain strong and safe. Essentially, they protect our money and our nation's economy.

A bank examiner's primary responsibilities are to ensure the safety and soundness of the bank he or she examines and to enforce the rules and regulations of the state or federal organization he or she represents. To accomplish this, bank examiners travel to different banks throughout the year. In most small- to medium-sized banks, they set up temporary offices. In larger banks, they may have permanent offices. The examination process can take anywhere from a few weeks to several months, depending on the size of the bank. A few extremely large banks are examined constantly throughout the year.

Bank examiners should not be confused with auditors or accountants. A bank examiner is as interested in a bank's operations as in the bank's financial records. Bank examiners conduct their examinations by reviewing a bank's policies to see, first of all, whether the policies are sound. They then review the bank's records to discover whether the bank is following its own policies. Bank examiners also observe the bank's day-to-day operations and interview managers and employees.

Ed Seifried, who served as a bank examiner within the OCC for more than 25 years, notes, "Bank examinations should involve dialogue and discussion. Banks may not like the process [of being examined], but they generally accept it if they feel that they are being assessed by people who treat them fairly and who understand banking."

Bank examiners usually work in teams under one *bank-examiner-in-charge*. Each member or group within a team studies a different area of the bank's operations. One person or group might study the bank's lending policies and procedures. Another might study the bank's asset management. Still others examine the bank's information technology or estate management. Different regulatory agencies examine different types of banks and different areas of operation. The *chief bank examiner* is responsible for assembling the team for each bank. The composition of these teams varies depending on the nature of each bank's business. Because banking practices today are so complex, many regulatory organizations design their examination strategy around a bank's greatest areas of risk. This so-called "supervision by risk" enables regulatory organizations to examine banks more frequently and with greater efficiency.

"Every examination is tailored to the individual bank," says Seifried. "The person in charge of the exam studies the bank in advance in order to develop an examination strategy."

Once a team of examiners has thoroughly reviewed different areas of a bank's operations, they analyze their findings, draw conclusions, and prepare a report. This report is forwarded to the regulatory agency for review. It is then returned to the bank's board of directors. These reports wield considerable power. A bank must act quickly to correct any problems identified in an examination. If a bank fails to do so, bank examiners have the authority to exact fines. In severe cases, a bank examiner can close banks or insist that they merge with other, more sound banks.

Because bank examiners must be able to exercise completely independent judgment about a bank's operations, their reports are strictly confidential. "The confidentiality is to ensure that there is no interference with the regulatory process," Seifried explains. "If bank examiners could be sued for rendering judgments, they might not be able to be as objective."

REQUIREMENTS

High School

If you are interested in entering this profession, you should begin laying a solid college prep foundation during high school. Take math courses, such as algebra and geometry, statistics, and business courses. Also, take as many computer courses as you can. You will be using computers throughout your career, and the more comfortable you are with this tool the better. You should also take English classes to develop good writing and communication skills. Researching, compiling reports, and presenting your findings will be a large part of your job as a bank examiner.

Postsecondary Training

After high school, the next step on your road to becoming a bank examiner is to get a college degree. Typical majors for this field include accounting, economics, business administration, commercial or banking law, or other business-related subjects. Once you have graduated from college, you may choose to work immediately for a regulatory agency or you may gain applied business experience by working, for example, for a financial institution. Either option is acceptable, though more and more regulatory agencies are actively recruiting candidates who have some business experience. Another possibility is to complete your education while working at the same time through such programs as the OCC's Bank Examiner Cooperative Education Program (see the Web site http://www.occ.treas. gov/jobs/coop.htm). Remember, though, that whatever route you pick, you won't become a full-fledged bank examiner overnight. Those who begin their careers working for a regulatory agency generally start as assistant or associate examiners. If you enter the field after gaining business experience, you may start at a higher-level position, but it will still take some time and training to become a bank examiner.

Regulatory agencies provide rigorous training for their bank examiners. Assistant bank examiners must take a series of courses and tests during their first several years as employees of a regulatory agency. They also gain on-the-job experience by working on examination teams. To become a bank examiner, you will need five or more years of experience in auditing or examining financial institutions. In addition, candidates with the best potential for advancement have experience with evaluating computer risk management in financial institutions. That is, they have a great deal of knowledge about assessing the security and flexibility of a financial institution's computer system.

Certification or Licensing

Some employers require their employees have or give promotion preference to employees with industry certifications, such as certified financial analyst or certified information systems auditor. In addition, bank examiners must be commissioned (approved) to examine banks only by a state or federal regulator before they can function as full-fledged examiners. This process typically takes five years. The Bank Administration Institute (BAI), an organization for financial professionals, also offers a number of courses that can help individuals prepare for careers as examiners.

Other Requirements

Successful bank examiners are committed to lifelong learning. Even after you have reached the position of bank examiner, it will be important to stay on top of new computer developments, laws and regulations, and changes in the field. Also, you should be able to work well with others since you will be working with teams of examiners as well as interacting with professionals at the financial institutions being examined. Be prepared to travel as part of your job; often you will be sent from one financial institution to another to perform examinations. Finally, if you enjoy detailed and analytical work with numbers, this may be the field for you.

EXPLORING

A good way to learn more about this field is by conducting information interviews with various banking professionals. You also should read all the literature banks produce in order to learn about different types of accounts and saving mechanisms.

College students should seek part-time jobs or internships within banks. Because bank examiners must be familiar with banking operations from the ground up, one of the best places for a college student to gain experience is by working as a teller in a bank.

EMPLOYERS

Approximately 26,000 financial examiners are employed in the United States. Almost all bank examiners are employees of federal or state governing agencies. They work for the OCC, the Federal Reserve System, the Office of Thrift Supervision, the FDIC, and many other federal and state agencies.

STARTING OUT

College graduates can enter this field via a number of avenues. The Office of Personnel Management (OPM) is the federal government's human resources department. The OPM maintains a list of job listings and also can provide information about requirements, benefits, and salaries. Visit http://www.usajobs.opm.gov for more information.

Someone interested in this work should also contact an agency such as the OCC directly and apply for openings. Most federal regulatory agencies, and many state agencies, maintain job hotlines and Web sites. (For examples on the Web, visit the Careers at the OCC page, http://www.occ.treas.gov/jobs/careers.htm, and the Careers at FDIC page, http://www.fdic.gov/about/jobs.)

A number of private newsletters available in print or online, such as *Federal Career Opportunities* (http://www.fedjobs.com) and *Federal Jobs Digest* (http://www.jobsfed.com) also list federal job openings.

ADVANCEMENT

Individuals usually enter this field as assistant examiners and, over the course of four to five years, progress to *commissioned examiners*. Commissioned examiners might be given responsibility for several small banks. As the examiner gains experience and establishes a

Mean Annual Earnings for
Financial Examiners by Industry, 2006

Federal Government	$94,820
Monetary Authorities-Central Bank	$79,110
Securities and Commodity Contracts Intermediation and Brokerage	$77,940
Depository Credit Intermediation	$63,920
Nondepository Credit Intermediation	$59,450
State Government	$56,970

Source: U.S. Department of Labor

reputation for integrity, insight, and thoroughness, he or she may be given responsibility for larger banks and larger teams of examiners. Examiners who handle larger banks also tend to earn more money.

After many years, an examiner may be offered a supervisory position. *Supervisors* usually stay in one office and are responsible for managing a large number of examiners who are working in the field.

Examiners also advance by moving to agencies that offer higher salary scales. Still others leave the profession entirely and put their skills to work as *banking consultants*. Because examiners study so many different banks, of varying degrees of soundness and efficiency, they can become highly successful, sought-after consultants.

EARNINGS

The U.S. Department of Labor reports the median annual wage of financial examiners was $65,370 in 2006, with 10 percent earning under $34,790 and 10 percent earning $118,000 or more. "Most experienced examiners earn about $60,000," notes Ed Seifried, "but it depends largely on where they want to end up. Supervisors can earn substantially more than that, but they also have additional responsibilities and pressures."

Most state and federal employees receive excellent benefits, such as health insurance, dental and vision coverage, life insurance, retirement packages, savings plans, sick leave, paid holidays, disability insurance, and child care allowance. The benefits for government employees tend to be extremely competitive and difficult to match in the private sector.

WORK ENVIRONMENT

A bank examiner is a nomadic creature, spending several weeks or months in each location before moving on. Bank examiners often work closely with teams of up to 30 or 40 other examiners who also are separated from their family and friends. Most examination teams develop a strong sense of camaraderie that sustains them during the weeks they must live out of hotels. To compensate for the travel, many regulatory agencies offer examiners an extra day off every other week. Examiners who work in these agencies work nine business days and take the 10th day off.

Bank examiners work in temporary offices, surrounded by professionals who may harbor ambiguous feelings about being examined. The work, however, can be interesting and rewarding.

"It can be a great job," says Ed Seifried. "I was with the OCC for more than 25 years and I spent 23 of those years in the field. I loved that part of it. When you're in the field, you are surrounded by knowledgeable people who have a strong interest in getting problems resolved. You also have a lot of interesting conversations."

OUTLOOK

The U.S. Department of Labor predicts that employment for financial examiners will grow about as fast as the average for all occupations through 2016. The banking industry is undergoing tremendous consolidation, and government regulations are changing. As more and more banks merge, fewer examiners may be needed at the state and federal levels. While there may be fewer new positions in this job, those who do enter the field can expect considerable job security. Employment in this field is usually not affected by general economic fluctuations. In addition, job openings will result from the need to replace those who retire or leave for other positions.

FOR MORE INFORMATION

The BAI is an organization for financial professionals offering such things as seminars, training courses, and Banking Strategies *magazine.*

Bank Administration Institute (BAI)
One North Franklin, Suite 1000
Chicago, IL 60606-3421
Tel: 888-284-4078
Email: info@bai.org
http://www.bai.org

The Federal Reserve System influences money and credit conditions in the United States, supervises and regulates banking, maintains the stability of the financial system, and provides certain financial services. For banking news, career opportunities, and publications, visit its Web site.

Board of Governors of the Federal Reserve System
20th Street and Constitution Avenue, NW
Washington, DC 20551-0001
Tel: 202-452-3000
http://www.federalreserve.gov

The Federal Deposit Insurance Corporation (FDIC) is responsible for maintaining public confidence in the nation's banking system. The FDIC provides deposit insurance for banks and savings associations. This resource can offer information about banking policies, regulations, and career opportunities.

Federal Deposit Insurance Corporation (FDIC)
3501 North Fairfax Drive
Arlington, VA 22226-3599
Tel: 877-275-3342
Email: publicinfo@fdic.gov
http://www.fdic.gov

The Federal Reserve Bank of Minneapolis is one of the 12 Federal Reserve Banks throughout the United States. This source can provide information about the economy, the history of banking in the United States, and career opportunities within the Federal Reserve.

Federal Reserve Bank of Minneapolis
90 Hennepin Avenue
Minneapolis, MN 55401-1804
Tel: 612-204-5000
http://woodrow.mpls.frb.fed.us

The Office of Personnel Management is the primary human resources center for the U.S. government. This resource can provide additional information about requirements, training, opportunities, and salaries.

Office of Personnel Management
1900 E Street, NW
Washington, DC 20415-1000
Tel: 202-606-1800
Email: General@opm.gov
http://www.opm.gov

The Office of the Comptroller of the Currency (OCC) supervises national banks to ensure a safe, sound, and competitive national banking system. This resource can offer information about the opportunities, training, requirements, and salary scale within the OCC.

Office of the Comptroller of the Currency (OCC)
Administrator of National Banks
Washington, DC 20219
Email: careers@occ.treas.gov
http://www.occ.treas.gov

The Office of Thrift Supervision (OTS) is the primary regulator of all federal and many state-chartered thrift institutions. This resource can offer information about the opportunities, training, requirements, and salary scale within the OTS.

Office of Thrift Supervision (OTS)
1700 G Street, NW
Washington, DC 20552-0003
Tel: 202-906-6000
Email: public.info@ots.treas.gov
http://www.ots.treas.gov

Bounty Hunters

OVERVIEW

Bounty hunters, also known as *bail enforcement agents* or *fugitive recovery agents,* track down and return individuals who are fugitives from justice. People who get arrested are often given the opportunity to post bail money so they can go free while waiting for a hearing or trial. When these people post the bail money, they are promising that they will return on the assigned court date. If they do not return on that date, they lose their bail money (or the bail bondsman loses his) and become fugitives from justice. Bounty hunters spend time researching and interviewing to get leads on the person they are tracking. Bounty hunters working in the United States account for thousands of arrests annually.

HISTORY

The history of the bail process dates back to English common law. People who were charged with crimes against the king were allowed to go free if someone else guaranteed that the individual would return. If that did not happen, the person who guaranteed the return of the individual often had to pay the price instead. In America, this process continued but gave birth to the modern bail bondsman and bounty hunter, who work together to ensure that accused people appear for hearings, trials, and sentences. Specifically, bounty hunting grew as a profession during the westward expansion of the United States. Because fugitives would often run as far west as possible to get away from local law enforcement, bounty hunters were often found tracking lawbreakers in the Old West. Though in many states fugitive-recovery activities have come to be

QUICK FACTS

School Subjects
English
Government

Personal Skills
Communication/ideas
Following instructions

Work Environment
Indoors and outdoors
Primarily multiple locations

Minimum Education Level
Some postsecondary training

Salary Range
$20,000 to $40,000 to
$100,000

Certification or Licensing
Required by certain states

Outlook
About as fast as the average

DOT
N/A

GOE
N/A

NOC
N/A

O*NET-SOC
N/A

performed by marshals, sheriffs, and detectives, the bail-bond system ensures that bounty hunters still flourish in the United States.

THE JOB

Bounty hunters work in conjunction with bail bondsmen and the court system. The scenario plays out as follows: An individual is arrested for breaking a law. The individual is given the chance to be freed from jail if he or she agrees to be at court on a certain date by posting a large amount of money. Most people who are arrested do not have these large sums of money on hand, so they enlist the services of a bail bondsman who provides the money to the court. The individual must pay the bondsman a fee—usually 10 percent of the actual posted bond. If the individual does not show up on the court date, the bondsman can either try to bring the person in or hire a bounty hunter to track the person down. The bounty hunter is paid only if the fugitive is returned to court.

After the bounty hunter is on the case, the main goal is to locate the fugitive as quickly and as safely as possible. Although the time frame varies from state to state and court to court, bail enforcement agents usually have 90 days at the most to bring back the fugitive. Locating a fugitive requires research, detection, and law enforcement skills. "Most of the time it takes time and patience," explains bail enforcement agent John Norman. "Many days are spent interviewing people, tracing paper trails, sitting in vehicles for countless hours of surveillance, just to await that moment to re-arrest this individual." Bounty hunters can use almost any means possible to re-arrest a fugitive. In most states they can enter the homes of fugitives if they believe, beyond a reasonable doubt, that the fugitive is inside. Sometimes the bounty hunter will interview family members or check the trash at the fugitive's home to find a clue as to where he or she has gone. Most bounty hunters use weapons to protect themselves and to persuade a fugitive to return peacefully. "The field can also be very dangerous," Norman cautions. "Getting shot at or knifed is not uncommon." After the fugitive is found, the bounty hunter makes a private arrest of the individual and takes the fugitive back to jail to await trial. "This process of retrieval can be easy sometimes and hard others," Norman adds. Although most bounty hunters re-arrest the fugitive themselves, some locate the fugitive and then alert the local law officials to make the actual arrest.

Bounty hunting is not all tracking people and bringing them back alive, however. Bounty hunting is a business, and like any other business, it must be run efficiently. In order to get work, bail enforcement agents must be able to advertise their services to become part of as many bail bondsmen "networks" as possible. Some bondsmen work with just a select few bounty hunters, while others send out their fugitive recovery requests to large networks of bounty hunters who compete against each other to bring back the fugitive. Because bounty hunters get paid only if they bring the person back, care must be taken to use resources wisely. Someone who spends $1,000 to find a fugitive with a reward for only $750 will not be in business long. Besides monetary resources, many bail enforcement agents have research assistants who work for them. Enforcement agents must be able to manage their employees in these situations. Bounty hunters also often work under contracts with law enforcement or bail bondsmen. They must be able to draw up contracts and be well-informed regarding all the legal aspects of those contracts.

REQUIREMENTS

High School

Although you will not find a class at school called Bounty Hunting 101, there are some courses that can help you prepare for a job in this field while you are still in high school. Classes in government, political science, communication, and business will help you prepare for the legal and business side of bounty hunting. Take self-defense or martial arts courses if you have the chance, as they can give you skills sometimes necessary in the apprehension of a fugitive. Foreign languages may come in handy as well, depending on the area of the country where you may be working.

Postsecondary Training

You are not required to have a college degree to be a bounty hunter. However, some postsecondary training is important for success and safety as a bail enforcement agent. "One way or another, you should have at least some sort of training in law enforcement and criminal justice," John Norman recommends. If a college degree or vocational school is in your future, aim for criminal justice studies or police academy training. If you want to focus immediately on bail enforcement, some training opportunities are available. The National Institute of Bail Enforcement and the National Association of Bail Enforcement Agents, for example, provide training seminars. (For contact information on these programs see the list at the end of this article.)

Certification or Licensing

Regulations covering bounty hunters' activities vary by state. It is, therefore, very important that you check with your state's attorney general's office, department of public safety, or professional licensing board to determine the rules for your area. In addition, it is important to be aware of other state's regulations in case your work takes you there. For example, some states, such as Illinois, prohibit bounty hunting. Some states, such as North Carolina, have as part of their requirements that "bail runners" work for only one bail bondsman or bail bond agency. Other states, such as Mississippi and Connecticut, have licensing requirements for bail enforcement agents; however, the licensing requirements themselves vary from state to state. And finally, some states, such as Georgia, have requirements such as registration with a sheriff's department or other agency. Generally, licensing involves passing a written test, passing a drug test and background check, being at least a certain age, being a U.S. citizen, and having completed some type of approved training. Anyone using a gun must, of course, have a license to do so.

Other Requirements
Bounty hunters must be able to handle high-stress situations that are often dangerous. Because of the nature of the work, the bounty hunter should be trained in the use of firearms and other weapons. Bounty hunters must be physically fit and able to defend themselves in dangerous situations.

EXPLORING

Bounty hunting can be dangerous, so you may be wondering how you can explore the field without getting hurt. That is a good question, but there are ways you can get an idea about the situations you would be encountering without being thrown into the thick of a fight. First, do some research. Contact your local and state authorities and ask for information about current laws and how they affect bounty hunters. With that information under your belt, you can contact your local police and ask to go on a ride-along with the specific focus on the times officers assist bounty hunters. (This "assistance" is usually just sitting in the patrol car to further persuade the fugitive that this is the real thing.) You may get the chance, from a safe distance, to watch the bounty hunter in action. Some cities and counties also conduct "citizen police academies" that train the public on many police situations and safety issues. Enroll in any programs you can find that provide this kind of information and training. Contact a bail bondsman (you will find many listed in the phone book) and find out if they are also bounty hunters. Ask any questions you may have. Try to interview several bondsmen to get a more balanced view of what it is like to work in the bail bonding and fugitive recovery business. As stated earlier, much of the bounty hunter's time is spent running the business. Join any clubs at school that focus on business, such as Junior Achievement.

EMPLOYERS

Most bounty hunters work independently. Many run their own businesses and contract their services to bail bondsmen and other individuals. Some bounty hunters are also bondsmen, and they combine the services into one business. These bounty hunters are part-timers, because most of their time is spent on bail bonding or investigating. "Some [bail enforcement agents] such as myself have their own companies," explains John Norman. "However, a lot of agents work directly under the bondsman. The bondsman is our main source of work in either case." Bondsmen either hire bounty hunters on a case-by-case basis or they hire them as full- or part-time employees. Some bounty hunters are also hired by private individuals for other services, such as recovering missing persons, finding persons who are not paying child support, and uncovering insurance fraud.

STARTING OUT

Although most bail enforcement agents own their own businesses, the majority start out working and learning the business from bail bondsmen or other bail enforcement agents. The best, most direct way to get started in the fugitive recovery field is to approach several bondsmen or bail enforcement agencies in your area. Most bounty hunters start out as *research assistants* or *skip tracers*. Skip tracers do the background and frontline interviewing to try to find the general location of the fugitive. The more training you have, the better chance you will have at landing that first job. You may have to start off in some form of law enforcement before you will be considered experienced or skilled enough to go into bounty hunting for a bondsman. Some starting points include jobs such as security guards, campus police, and researchers for private investigators.

ADVANCEMENT

Because most bail enforcement agents own their own agencies, they are at the top of their business with no higher position to be had.

However, because of the competition within the fugitive recovery field, there is a drive to be the "best of the best" and have the highest fugitive recovery rate. Bail enforcement agents want to be able to maintain and advertise a very high rate of return, and the best and highest-paid in the field are able to produce more than 90 percent of the fugitives they track. Many bail enforcement agents chase the goal of perfection as strongly as they chase each fugitive.

Bounty hunters who work for other bail enforcement agents or bondsmen can work toward owning their own agency. Usually success in tracking down fugitives is the path toward the recognition and marketability necessary to start a new fugitive recovery business.

EARNINGS

The bounty hunting business, like any other, takes time to develop, and bounty hunters who start their own agencies have many out-of-pocket expenses for items such as handcuffs and advertising. Some may end up losing money or only earning enough to break even. For those who manage to build up a business, however, earnings can be quite good. The National Center for Policy Analysis' 2000 report *Privatizing Probation and Parole* states that bounty hunters generally earn between $20,000 and $30,000 for part-time work. A 2001 article on the CNNMoney Web site notes that while most bonds are fairly small (meaning that a bounty hunter does not earn much from one recovery), annual incomes can be good because there are plenty of fugitives on the run and lots of work is available. According to CNNMoney, bounty hunters generally earn between $40,000 and $60,000 per year. It is important to note, however, that in this business earnings can vary greatly from month to month, depending on how many fugitives the bounty hunter is able to bring in, the bail bond for these fugitives, and expenses incurred in the process. Well-established bail enforcement agents with excellent reputations often get the highest-paying cases, such as for a fugitive who has run on a $100,000 bail, and may find their yearly earnings approaching the hundred thousand dollar mark.

Because they own their own businesses, most bail enforcement agents do not receive medical benefits. A few who work for well-established agencies may receive some types of benefits, but it is not the norm for the field. "In this business, sometimes it is slow or there is no business and there are lengthy times between paychecks. There are also no benefits like pensions, insurance, or things of that nature in most cases," says John Norman.

WORK ENVIRONMENT

Bounty hunters spend much of their time traveling in search of a fugitive or waiting for hours for a fugitive to appear. Because apprehending a fugitive is easiest in the middle of the night or early morning, the bounty hunter keeps odd hours and may work especially long hours when close to capturing a fugitive. A bail enforcement agent works on an as-needed basis, so there may be stretches of inactivity depending on the bondsman's needs for service. The number of hours worked varies with the number of fugitives being sought at any one time and the amount of time remaining to bring the fugitive in. Bounty hunters are often in perilous situations where injury or even death is a possibility. John Norman describes bail enforcement as a "painstaking, unforgiving business."

OUTLOOK

Employment for bounty hunters is increasing about as fast as the average for all other occupations, although this field has a narrow niche in the bail bonding business. Competition among bail enforcement agents continues to propel the field as a profession and as an asset to our legal system. Because bail bond agents and bail enforcement agents are working in private business, there is no cost to the taxpayer for the apprehension of these fugitives (as there would be if, for example, police officers worked exclusively on these cases). Another benefit of the private bail enforcement agent system is its high success rate (some professionals estimate it at 85 percent) for recovery of fugitives. Given the large percentage of recoveries and the lack of cost to local government, the future looks good for this profession. The ability of bail enforcement agents to work successfully within the parameters of the law should keep this field growing steadily in the future.

FOR MORE INFORMATION

Visit the Bail Bond Recovery Resource Center of The National Association of Investigative Specialists Web site. The resource center has information on the work of bounty hunters, laws affecting bounty hunting, and training materials.
  Bail Bond Recovery Resource Center
  The National Association of Investigative Specialists
  PO Box 33244
  Austin, TX 78764-0244

Tel: 512-719-3595
http://www.pimall.com/nais/bailr.html

For training information, visit NABEA's Web site.
National Association of Bail Enforcement Agents (NABEA)
PO Box 129
Falls Church, VA 22040-0129
Tel: 703-534-4211
http://www.nabea.org

For industry information, contact
National Enforcement Agency
PO Box 3540
Gaithersburg, MD 20885-3540
Tel: 866-384-4848
http://nationalbailenforcement.com

For information about fugitive recovery seminars, contact
National Institute of Bail Enforcement
PO Box 667
Spring Grove, IL 60081-0667
Tel: 815-675-0260
http://www.bounty-hunter.net

Corrections Officers

OVERVIEW

Corrections officers guard people who have been arrested and are awaiting trial or who have been tried, convicted, and sentenced to serve time in a penal institution. They search prisoners and their cells for weapons, drugs, and other contraband; inspect windows, doors, locks, and gates for signs of tampering; observe the conduct and behavior of inmates to prevent disturbances or escapes; and make verbal or written reports to superior officers. Corrections officers assign work to inmates and supervise their activities. They guard prisoners who are being transported between jails, courthouses, mental institutions, or other destinations, and supervise prisoners receiving visitors. When necessary, these workers use weapons or force to maintain discipline and order. There are approximately 500,000 corrections officers employed in the United States.

HISTORY

For centuries, punishment for criminal behavior was generally left in the hands of the injured individual or his or her relatives. This resulted in blood feuds, which could carry on for years and which eventually could be resolved by the payment of money to the victim or the victim's family. When kingdoms emerged as the standard form of government, certain actions came to be regarded as an affront to the king or the peace of his domain, and the king assumed the responsibility for punishing the wrongs committed by a subject or his clan. In this way, crime became a public offense. The earliest corrections officers were more likely to be executioners and torturers than guards or jailers.

Early criminals were treated inhumanely. They were often put to death for minor offenses, exiled, forced into hard labor, given corporal punishment, tortured, mutilated, turned into slaves, or left to rot in dungeons. Jailing criminals was not considered a penalty in and of itself, but rather as a temporary measure until punishment could be carried out. More often, prisons were established to punish debtors or to house orphans and delinquent youths. One of the earliest debtor's prisons was Bridewell, in London, England, which was established in 1553. Other European countries built similar institutions.

During the Enlightenment of the 18th century, the belief that punishment alone deters crime began to weaken. The practice of imprisonment became more and more common as attempts were made to fit the degree of punishment to the nature of the crime. Societies looked to deter crime with the promise of clear and just punishment. Rehabilitation of offenders was to be achieved through isolation, hard labor, penitence, and discipline. By 1829, prisoners in most prisons were required to perform hard labor, which proved more cost-effective for the prison systems. Before long, the rehabilitation aspect of imprisonment became less important than the goal of simply isolating prisoners from society and creating respect for authority and order. Prisoners were subjected to harsh treatment from generally untrained personnel.

By 1870, calls for prison reform introduced new sentencing procedures such as parole and probation. It was hoped that providing opportunities for early release would provide prisoners with more incentive toward rehabilitation. Prisons evolved into several types, providing minimum, medium, and maximum security. The role of the prison guard at each institution evolved accordingly. The recognition of prisoners' rights also provided new limitations and purposes for the conduct and duties of the prison guard. Corrections officers began to receive specialized training in the treatment and rehabilitation of prisoners.

Until the 1980s, corrections officers were employees of the federal, state, or local government. A dramatic increase in the number of prisoners meant overcrowded prisons and skyrocketing costs. At the same time, the system itself came under attack, especially the concepts of parole and reduced sentencing. Many states began to contract private companies to build and operate additional correctional facilities. Today, corrections officers are employed at every level of government and often by these private companies.

THE JOB

To prevent disturbances or escapes, corrections officers carefully observe inmates' conduct and behavior at all times. They watch for forbidden activities and infractions of the rules, as well as for poor attitudes or unsatisfactory adjustment to prison life. They try to settle disputes before violence can erupt. They may search the prisoners or their living quarters for weapons or drugs and inspect locks, bars on windows and doors, and gates for any evidence of tampering. The inmates are under guard constantly while eating, sleeping, exercising, bathing, and working. They are counted periodically to be sure all are present. Some officers are stationed on towers and at gates to prevent escapes. All rule violations and anything out of the ordinary are reported to a superior officer such as a chief jailer. In case of a major disturbance, corrections officers may use weapons or force to restore order.

Corrections officers give work assignments to prisoners, supervise them as they carry out their duties, and instruct them in unfamiliar tasks. Corrections officers are responsible for the physical needs of the prisoners, such as providing or obtaining meals and medical aid. They assure the health and safety of the inmates by checking the cells for unsanitary conditions and fire hazards.

These workers may escort inmates from their cells to the prison's visiting room, medical office, or chapel. Certain officers, called *patrol conductors,* guard prisoners who are being transported between courthouses, prisons, mental institutions, or other destinations, either by van, car, or public transportation. Officers at a penal institution may also screen visitors at the entrance and accompany them to other areas within the facility. From time to time, they may inspect mail addressed to prisoners, checking for contraband, help investigate crimes committed within the prison, or aid in the search for escapees.

Some police officers specialize in guarding juvenile offenders being held at a police station house or detention room pending a hearing, transfer to a correctional institution, or return to their parents. They often investigate the backgrounds of first offenders to check for a criminal history or to make a recommendation to the magistrate regarding disposition of the case. Lost or runaway children are also placed in the care of these officers until their parents or guardians can be located.

Immigration guards guard aliens held by the immigration service awaiting investigation, deportation, or release. *Gate tenders* check the identification of all persons entering and leaving the penal institution.

In most correctional institutions, *psychologists* and *social workers* are employed to counsel inmates with mental and emotional problems. It is an important part of a corrections officer's job, however, to supplement this with informal counseling. Officers may help inmates adjust to prison life, prepare for return to civilian life, and avoid committing crimes in the future. On a more immediate level, they may arrange for an inmate to visit the library, help inmates get in touch with their families, suggest where to look for a job after release from prison, or discuss personal problems. In some institutions, corrections officers may lead more formal group counseling sessions. As they fulfill more rehabilitative roles, corrections officers are increasingly required to possess a college-level education in psychology, criminology, or related areas of study.

Corrections officers keep a daily record of their activities and make regular reports, either verbal or written, to their supervisors. These reports concern the behavior of the inmates and the quality and quantity of work they do, as well as any disturbances, rule violations, and unusual occurrences that may have taken place.

Head corrections officers supervise and coordinate other corrections officers. They perform roll call and assign duties to the officers; direct the activities of groups of inmates; arrange the release and transfer of prisoners in accordance with a court order; maintain security and investigate disturbances among the inmates; maintain prison records and prepare reports; and review and evaluate the performance of their subordinates.

In small communities, corrections officers (who are sometimes called *jailers*) may also act as deputy sheriffs or police officers when they are not occupied with guard duties.

REQUIREMENTS

High School

To work as a corrections officer, candidates generally must meet the minimum age requirement—usually 18 or 21—and have a high school diploma or its equivalent. Individuals without a high school education may be considered for employment if they have qualifying work experience, such as probation and parole experience.

Postsecondary Training

Many states and correctional facilities prefer or require officers to have postsecondary training in psychology, criminology, or related areas of study. Some states require applicants to have one or two years of previous experience in corrections or related police work. Military experience or related work experience is also required by some state governments. On the federal level, applicants should have at least two years of college or two years of work or military experience.

Training for corrections officers ranges from the special academy instruction provided by the federal government in some states to the informal, on-the-job training furnished by most states and local governments. The Federal Bureau of Prisons operates a training center in Glynco, Georgia, where new hires generally undergo a three-week program of basic corrections education. Training academies have programs that last from four to eight weeks and instruct trainees on institutional policies, regulations, and procedures; the behavior and custody of inmates; security measures; and report writing. Training in self-defense, the use of firearms and other weapons, and emergency medical techniques is often provided. On-the-job trainees spend two to six months or more under the supervision of an experienced officer. During that period of time, they receive in-house training while gaining actual experience. Periodically, corrections officers may be given additional training as new ideas and procedures in criminal justice are developed.

Certification or Licensing
Numerous certification programs are available to corrections officers; these are optional in most states. Common certifications include self-defense, weapons use, urine analysis, shield and gun, shotgun/handgun, CPR, and cell extraction. Many officers also take advantage of additional training that is offered at their facility, such as suicide prevention, AIDS awareness, use of four-point restraints, and emergency preparedness. At most prisons, there is annual mandatory in-service training that focuses on policies and procedures. The American Correctional Association and the American Jail Association offer certification programs to corrections officers and corrections managers.

Corrections officers who work for the federal government and most state governments are covered by civil service systems or merit boards and may be required to pass a competitive exam for employment. Many states require random or comprehensive drug testing of their officers, either during hiring procedures or while employed at the facility.

Other Requirements
There is no denying that handling the inherent stress of this line of work takes a unique person. In a maximum-security facility, the environment is often noisy, crowded, poorly ventilated, and even dangerous. Corrections officers need the physical and emotional strength to handle the stress involved in working with criminals, some of whom may be violent. A corrections officer has to stay alert and aware of prisoners' actions and attitudes. This constant vigilance can be harder on some people. Work in a minimum-security prison is usually more comfortable, cleaner, and less stressful.

Corrections officers escort a prisoner into a courtroom. *(Syracuse Newspapers, Stephen Cannarelli, The Image Works)*

Officers need to use persuasion rather than brute force to get inmates to follow the rules. Certain inmates take a disproportionate amount of time and attention because they are either violent, mentally ill, or victims of abuse by other inmates. Officers have to carry out routine duties while being alert for the unpredictable outbursts. Sound judgment and the ability to think and act quickly are important qualities for corrections officers. With experience and training, corrections officers are usually able to handle volatile situations without resorting to physical force.

The ability to communicate clearly verbally and in writing is extremely important. Corrections officers have to write a number of reports, documenting routine procedures as well as any violations by the inmates. A correction officer's eight-hour shift can easily extend to 10 hours because of the reports that must be written.

An effective corrections officer is not easily intimidated or influenced by the inmates. While it's true that a person needs some physical strength to perform the job, corrections officers also need to be able to use their head to anticipate and defuse any potentially dangerous situations between inmates or between guards and inmates.

Most correctional institutions require candidates to be at least 18 years old (sometimes 21 years old), have a high school diploma, and be a U.S. citizen with no criminal record. There are also health and physical strength requirements, and many states have minimum height, vision, and hearing standards. Other common requirements are a driver's license and a job record that shows that they've been dependable.

EXPLORING

Because of age requirements and the nature of the work, there are no opportunities for high school students to gain actual experience while still in school. Where the minimum age requirement is 21, prospective corrections officers may prepare for employment by taking college courses in criminal justice or police science. Enrollment in a two- or four-year college degree program in a related field is encouraged. Military service may also offer experience and training in corrections. Social work is another way to gain experience. You may also look into obtaining a civilian job as a clerk or other worker for the police department or other protective service organization. Related part-time, volunteer, or summer work may also be available in psychiatric hospitals and other institutions providing physical and emotional counseling and services. Many online services also have forums for corrections officers and other public safety employees, and these may provide opportunities to read about and communicate with people active in this career.

EMPLOYERS

Most corrections officers work for the government at the local, state, and federal levels in penal institutions and in jobs connected with the penal system. Of the approximately 500,000 corrections officers employed in the United States, roughly 60 percent work in state-run correctional facilities such as prisons, prison camps, and reformatories. Most of the rest are employed at city and county jails or other institutions. Roughly 18,000 work for the federal government and approximately 16,000 are employed by private corrections contractors.

STARTING OUT

To apply for a job as a corrections officer, contact federal or state civil service commissions, state departments of correction, or local correctional facilities and ask for information about entrance requirements, training, and job opportunities. Private contractors and other companies are also a growing source of employment opportunities.

Books to Read

Allen, Harry E., Edward J. Latessa, Bruce S. Ponder, and Clifford E. Simonsen. *Corrections in America: An Introduction.* 11th ed. Upper Saddle River, N.J.: Prentice Hall, 2006.

Clear, Todd R., George F. Cole, and Michael D. Reisig. *American Corrections.* 8th ed. Belmont, Calif.: Wadsworth Publishing, 2008.

Cornelius, Gary F. *Stressed Out: Strategies for Living and Working in Corrections.* 2d ed. Alexandria, Va.: American Correctional Association, 2005.

Cromwell, Paul, ed. *In Their Own Words: Criminals on Crime.* 4th ed. Los Angeles, Calif.: Roxbury Publishing Company, 2005.

Muraskin, Roslyn. *Key Correctional Issues.* Upper Saddle River, N.J.: Prentice Hall, 2004.

Stinchcomb, Jeanne B. *Corrections: Past, Present and Future.* Alexandria, Va.: American Correctional Association, 2005.

Many officers enter this field from social work areas and parole and probation positions.

ADVANCEMENT

Many officers take college courses in law enforcement or criminal justice to increase their chances of promotion. In some states, officers must serve two years in each position before they can be considered for a promotion.

With additional education and training, experienced officers can also be promoted to supervisory or administrative positions such as head corrections officer, *assistant warden,* or *prison director.* Officers who want to continue to work directly with offenders can move into various other positions. For example, *probation and parole officers* monitor and counsel offenders, process their release from prison, and evaluate their progress in becoming productive members of society. *Recreation leaders* organize and instruct offenders in sports, games, and arts and crafts.

EARNINGS

Wages for corrections officers vary considerably depending on their employers and their level of experience. According to the U.S. Department of Labor, the 2006 mean annual earnings for corrections officers employed by the federal government were $48,000; for those employed by state governments, $38,960; and for those employed by local governments, $37,330. The U.S. Department of Labor reports that overall the lowest paid 10 percent of corrections officers earned less than $23,600 per year in 2006, and the highest paid 10 percent earned more than $58,580. Median earnings for corrections officers were $35,760.

The U.S. Department of Labor reports higher earnings for supervisors/managers, with a median yearly income of $52,580 in 2006. The lowest paid 10 percent earned less than $33,270, and the highest paid 10 percent earned more than $81,230.

Overtime, night shift, weekend, and holiday pay differentials are generally available at most institutions. Fringe benefits may include health, disability, and life insurance; uniforms or a cash allowance to buy their own uniforms; and sometimes meals and housing. Officers who work for the federal government and for most state governments are covered by civil service systems or merit boards. Some corrections officers also receive retirement and pension plans, and retirement is often possible after 20 to 25 years of service.

WORK ENVIRONMENT

Because prison security must be maintained around the clock, work schedules for corrections officers may include nights, weekends, and holidays. The workweek, however, generally consists of five days, eight hours per day, except during emergencies, when many officers work overtime.

Corrections officers may work indoors or outdoors, depending on their duties. Conditions can vary even within an institution: Some areas are well lighted, ventilated, and temperature-controlled, while others are overcrowded, hot, and noisy. Officers who work outdoors, of course, are subject to all kinds of weather. Correctional institutions occasionally present unpredictable or even hazardous situations. If violence erupts among the inmates, corrections officers may be in danger of injury or death. Although this risk is higher than for most other occupations, corrections work is usually routine.

Corrections officers need physical and emotional strength to cope with the stress inherent in dealing with criminals, many of whom may be dangerous or incapable of change. A corrections officer has to remain alert and aware of the surroundings, prisoners' movements and attitudes, and any potential for danger or violence. Such continual, heightened levels of alertness often create psychological stress for some workers. Most institutions have stress-reduction programs or seminars for their employees, but if not, insurance usually covers some form of therapy for work-related stress.

OUTLOOK

Employment in this field is expected to grow faster than the average for all occupations through 2016, according to the U.S. Department of Labor. There should be thousands of job openings annually for qualified workers. The ongoing prosecution of illegal drugs, new tough-on-crime legislation, and increasing mandatory sentencing policies will create a need for more prison beds and more corrections officers. The extremely crowded conditions in today's correctional institutions have created a need for more corrections officers to guard the inmates more closely and relieve the tensions. A greater number of officers will also be required as a result of the expansion or new construction of facilities. As prison sentences become longer through mandatory minimum sentences set by state law, the number of prisons needed will increase. In addition, many job openings will occur from a characteristically high turnover rate, as well as from the need to fill vacancies caused by the death or retirement of older workers. Traditionally, correction agencies have difficulty attracting qualified employees due to job location and salary considerations.

Some states are reconsidering their mandatory sentencing guidelines "because of budgetary constraints, court decisions, and doubts about their effectiveness," according to the U.S. Department of Labor. This may limit employment growth for corrections officers in some states.

Because security must be maintained at correctional facilities at all times, corrections officers can depend on steady employment. They are not usually affected by poor economic conditions or changes in government spending. Corrections officers are rarely laid off, even when budgets need to be trimmed. Instead, because of high turnovers, staffs can be cut simply by not replacing those officers who leave.

Most jobs will be found in relatively large institutions located near metropolitan areas, although opportunities for corrections officers exist in jails and other smaller facilities throughout the country. The increasing use of private companies and privately run prisons may limit the growth of jobs in this field as these companies are more likely to keep a close eye on the bottom line. Use of new technologies, such as surveillance equipment, automatic gates, and other devices, may also allow institutions to employ fewer officers.

FOR MORE INFORMATION

For information on certification, training, conferences, and membership, contact
American Correctional Association
206 North Washington Street, Suite 200
Alexandria, VA 22314-2528
Tel: 703-224-0000
http://www.aca.org

American Jail Association
1135 Professional Court
Hagerstown, MD 21740-5853
Tel: 301-790-3930
http://www.aja.org

American Probation and Parole Association
2760 Research Park Drive
Lexington, KY 405111-8410
Tel: 859-244-8203
Email: appa@csg.org
http://www.appa-net.org

For information on entrance requirements, training, and career opportunities for corrections officers at the federal level, contact
Federal Bureau of Prisons
320 First Street, NW
Washington, DC 20534-0002
Tel: 202-307-3198
http://www.bop.gov

For information about the corrections industry, visit
The Corrections Connection
http://www.corrections.com

Court Reporters

QUICK FACTS

School Subjects
English
Foreign language
Government

Personal Skills
Communication/ideas
Following instructions

Work Environment
Primarily indoors
Primarily multiple locations

Minimum Education Level
Some postsecondary training

Salary Range
$23,430 to $45,610 to
$77,770+

Certification or Licensing
Recommended (certification)
Required by certain states
(licensing)

Outlook
Much faster than the average

DOT
202

GOE
09.07.02

NOC
1244

O*NET-SOC
23-2091.00

OVERVIEW

Court reporters record every word at hearings, trials, depositions, and other legal proceedings. Most court reporters transcribe the notes of the proceedings by using computer-aided transcription systems that print out regular, legible copies of the proceedings. The court reporter must also edit and proofread the final transcript and create the official transcript of the trial or other legal proceeding. Approximately 19,000 court reporters work in the United States.

HISTORY

To record legal proceedings, court reporters use shorthand, a system of abbreviated writing that has its beginnings in script forms developed more than 2,000 years ago. Ancient Greeks and Romans used symbols and letters to record poems, speeches, and political meetings.

Europeans, such as the Englishman Timothy Bright, began to develop systems of shorthand in the 15th and 16th centuries. These systems were refined throughout the 17th and 18th centuries. Shorthand was used primarily in personal correspondence and for copying or creating literary works.

Shorthand was applied to business communications after the invention of the typewriter. The stenotype, the first shorthand machine, was invented by an American court reporter in 1910. Before the introduction of Dictaphones, tape recorders, and other electronic recording devices, shorthand was the fastest and most accurate way for a secretary or reporter to copy down what was being said at a business meeting or other event. Court reporters today still use stenotype machines, but they use computer-aided transcription to translate the stenographic symbols into English text. Computer-aided transcription (CAT) saves the court reporter time that can be better used editing and refining the text.

More than 90 percent of court reporters use computers in their work, according to the National Court Reporters Association. Computers allow court reporters to offer more services to lawyers and judges, such as condensed transcripts (an extra transcript that fits several pages of testimony on one page), concordant indexes (indexes each word in a transcript by page and line number), and keyword indexes (indexes certain important terms as requested by the lawyer). More than 25 percent of court reporters use the Internet for research, advertising, and connecting with clients, according to the *Journal of Court Reporting.*

THE JOB

Court reporters are best known as the men or women sitting in the courtroom silently typing to record what is said by everyone involved. While that is true, it is only part of the court reporter's job. Much more work is done after the court reporter leaves the trial or hearing.

In the courtroom, court reporters use symbols or shorthand forms of complete words to record what is said as quickly as it is spoken on a stenotype machine that looks like a miniature typewriter. The stenotype machine has 24 keys on its keyboard. Each key prints a single symbol. Unlike a typewriter, however, the court reporter using a stenotype machine can press more than one key at a time to print different combinations of symbols. Each symbol or combination represents a different sound, word, or phrase. As testimony is given, the reporter strikes one or more keys to create a phonetic representation of the testimony on a strip of paper, as well as on a computer hard drive inside the stenotype machine. The court reporter later uses a computer to translate and transcribe the testimony into legible, full-page documents or stores them for reference. People in court may speak at a rate of between 250 and 300 words a minute, and court reporters must record this testimony word for word and quickly.

Accurate recording of a trial is vital because the court reporter's record becomes the official transcript for the entire proceeding. In our legal system, court transcripts can be used after the trial for many important purposes. If a legal case is appealed, for example, the court reporter's transcript becomes the foundation for any further legal action. The appellate judge refers to the court reporter's transcript to see what happened in the trial and how the evidence was presented.

Because of the importance of accuracy, a court reporter who misses a word or phrase must interrupt the proceedings to have the words repeated. The court reporter may be asked by the judge to read aloud a portion of recorded testimony during the trial to refresh everyone's memory. Court reporters must pay close attention to all the proceedings and be able to hear and understand everything. Sometimes it may be difficult to understand a particular witness or attorney due to poor diction, a strong accent, or a soft speaking voice. Nevertheless, the court reporter cannot be shy about stopping the trial and asking for clarification.

Court reporters must be adept at recording testimony on a wide range of legal issues, from medical malpractice to income tax evasion. In some cases, court reporters may record testimony at a murder trial or a child-custody case. Witnessing tense situations and following complicated arguments are unavoidable parts of the job. The court reporter must be able to remain detached from the drama that unfolds in court while faithfully recording all that is said.

After the trial or hearing, the court reporter has more work to do. Using a CAT program, the stenotype notes are translated to English. The majority of these translated notes are accurate. This rough translation is then edited either by the court reporter or by a *scopist*—an assistant to the court reporter who edits and cleans up the notes. If a stenotype note did not match a word in the court reporter's CAT dictionary during translation, it shows up still in stenotype form. The court reporter must manually change these entries into words and update the dictionary used in translating. If there are any meanings of words or spellings of names that are unfamiliar to the court reporter, research must be done to verify that the correct term or spelling is used. The court reporter then proofreads the transcript to check for any errors in meaning, such as the word *here* instead of the word *hear*. If necessary or requested by the lawyer or judge, special indexes and concordances are compiled using computer programs. The last step the court reporter must take is printing and binding the transcript to make it an organized and usable document for the lawyers and judge.

In some states, the court reporter is responsible for swearing in the witnesses and documenting items of evidence.

In addition to the traditional method of court reporting discussed above, a number of other methods of reporting have emerged in recent years. In real-time court reporting, the court reporter types the court proceedings on a stenotype machine, which is connected to a computer. The symbols that the court reporter types on the stenotype machine are converted to words that can be read by those involved in the case. This process is known as Communication Access Realtime Translation (CART). In addition to its use in court, CART is used in meetings, educational settings, and for closed captioning for the hearing-impaired on television.

In electronic reporting, the court reporter uses audio equipment to record court proceedings. The court reporter is responsible for overseeing the recording process, taking notes to identify speakers and clarify other issues, and ensuring the quality of the recording. Court reporters who specialize in this method are often asked to create a written transcript of the recorded proceeding.

In voice writing, a court reporter wears a hand-held mask (known as a voice silencer) that is equipped with a microphone. The reporter repeats the testimony of all parties involved in the trial while holding the mask to his or her face. Some reporters translate the voice recording in real time using computer speech recognition technology. Others wait till after the proceedings to create the translation using voice recognition technology or by doing the translation manually.

REQUIREMENTS

High School

To be a court reporter, you need to have a high school diploma or its equivalent. Take as many high-level classes in English as you can and get a firm handle on grammar and spelling. Take typing classes and computer classes to give you a foundation in using computers and a head start in keyboarding skills. Classes in government and business will be helpful as well. Training in Latin can also be a great benefit because it will help you understand the many medical and legal terms that arise during court proceedings. Knowledge of foreign languages can also be helpful because as a court reporter, you will often transcribe the testimony of non-English speakers with the aid of court-appointed translators.

Postsecondary Training

Court reporters are required to complete a specialized training program in shorthand reporting. These programs usually last between two and four years and include instruction on how to enter at least 225 words a minute on a stenotype machine. Other topics include computer operations, transcription methods, English grammar, and the principles of law. For court cases involving medical issues, students must also take courses on human anatomy and physiology. Basic medical and legal terms are also explained.

About 130 postsecondary schools and colleges have two- and four-year programs in court reporting; approximately 70 of these programs are approved by the National Court Reporters Association (NCRA). Many business colleges offer these programs. As a court reporting student in these programs, you must master machine shorthand, or stenotyping, and real-time reporting. The NCRA states that to graduate from one of these programs, you must be able to type at least 225 words per minute and pass tests that gauge your written knowledge and speed.

Certification or Licensing

The NCRA offers several levels of certification for its members. To receive the registered professional reporter certification, you must pass tests that are administered twice a year at more than 100 sites in the United States and overseas. The registered merit reporter certification means you have passed an exam with speeds up to 260 words per minute. The registered diplomate reporter certification is obtained by passing a knowledge exam. This certification shows that the court reporter has gained valuable professional knowledge and experience through years of reporting. The certified realtime reporter certification is given to reporters who have obtained the specialized skill of converting the spoken word into written word within seconds. Several other specialized certifications are available for the court reporter.

The American Association of Electronic Reporters and Transcribers offers the following voluntary certifications: certified electronic court reporter, certified electronic court transcriber, and certified electronic court reporter and transcriber. The National Verbatim Reporters Association offers the following voluntary certifications: certified verbatim reporter, certificate of merit, and real-time verbatim reporter. Contact these organizations for information on requirements for each certification.

Some states require reporters to be notary publics or to be licensed through a state certification exam. Currently, more than 40 states grant licenses in either shorthand reporting or court reporting, although not all of these states require a license to work as a court reporter. Licenses are granted after the court reporter passes state examinations and fulfills any prerequisites (usually an approved shorthand reporting program).

Other Requirements

Because part of a court reporter's work is done within the confines of a courtroom, the ability to work under pressure is a must. Court reporters need to be able to meet deadlines with accuracy and atten-

A court reporter uses her keyboard and computer to record in real time the proceedings at a trial. *(Amelia Kunhardt, The Image Works)*

tion to detail. As stated previously, a court reporter must be highly skilled at the stenotype machine. A minimum of 225 words per minute is expected from a beginning court reporter.

Court reporters must be familiar with a wide range of medical and legal terms and must be assertive enough to ask for clarification if a term or phrase goes by without the reporter understanding it. Court reporters must be as unbiased as possible and accurately record what is said, not what they believe to be true. Patience and perfectionism are vital characteristics, as is the ability to work closely with judges and other court officials.

EXPLORING

To get an idea of what a court reporter does—at least the work they do in public—attend some trials at your local courts. Instead of focusing on the main players—witnesses, lawyers, judges—keep an eye on the court reporter. If you can, watch several reporters in different courtrooms under different judges to get a perspective on what the average court reporter does. Try to arrange a one-on-one meeting with a court reporter so you can ask the questions you really want answers for. Maybe you can convince one of your teachers to arrange a field trip to a local court.

EMPLOYERS

Approximately 19,000 court reporters are employed in the United States. Many court reporters are employed by city, county, state, or federal courts. Others work for themselves as freelancers or as employees of freelance reporting agencies. These freelance reporters are hired by attorneys to record the pretrial statements, or depositions, of experts and other witnesses. When people want transcripts of other important discussions, freelance reporters may be called on to record what is said at business meetings, large conventions, or similar events.

Most court reporters work in middle- to large-size cities, although they are needed anywhere a court of law is in session. In smaller cities, a court reporter may only work part time.

A new application of court-reporting skills and technology is in the field of television captioning. Using specialized computer-aided transcription systems, reporters can produce captions for live television events, including sporting events and national and local news, for the benefit of hearing-impaired viewers.

STARTING OUT

After completing the required training, court reporters usually work for a freelance reporting company that provides court reporters for business meetings and courtroom proceedings on a temporary basis. Qualified reporters can also contact these freelance reporting companies on their own. Occasionally a court reporter will be hired directly out of school as a courtroom official, but ordinarily only those with several years of experience are hired for full-time judiciary work. A would-be court reporter may start out working as a medical transcriptionist or other specific transcriptionist to get the necessary experience.

Career services counselors at community colleges can be helpful in finding that first job. The Internet is also rich with job boards and employment information for all careers, including court reporting.

ADVANCEMENT

Skilled court reporters may be promoted to a larger court system or to an otherwise more demanding position, with an accompanying increase in pay and prestige. Those working for a freelance company may be hired permanently by a city, county, state, or federal court. Those with experience working in a government position may choose to become a freelance court reporter and thereby have greater job flexibility and perhaps earn more money. Those with the necessary training, experience, and business skills may decide to open their own freelance reporting company.

According to a study funded by the National Court Reporters Foundation, court reporters advance by assuming more responsibility and greater skill levels; that gives the court reporter credibility in the eyes of the professionals in the legal system. Those advanced responsibilities include real-time reporting, coding and cross-referencing the official record, assisting others in finding specific information quickly, and helping the judge and legal counsel with procedural matters.

Court reporters can also follow alternative career paths as captioning experts, legal and medical transcriptionists, and cyber-conference moderators.

EARNINGS

Earnings vary according to the skill, speed, and experience of the court reporter, as well as geographic location. Those who are employed by large court systems generally earn more than their counterparts in smaller communities. The median annual income for all court reporters was $45,610 in 2006, according to the U.S. Department of Labor. Ten percent of reporters were paid less than $23,430 annually in 2006, and 10 percent had annual earnings of more than $77,770. Incomes can be even higher depending on the reporter's skill level, length of service, and the amount of time the reporter works. Official court reporters not only earn a salary, but also a per-page fee for transcripts. Freelance court reporters are paid by the job and also per page for transcripts.

Court reporters who work in small communities or as freelancers may not be able to work full-time. Successful court reporters with jobs in business environments may earn more than those in courtroom settings, but such positions carry less job security.

Those working for the government or full-time for private companies usually receive health insurance and other benefits, such as paid vacations and retirement pensions. Freelancers may or may not receive health insurance or other benefits, depending on the policies of their agencies.

WORK ENVIRONMENT

Offices and courtrooms are usually pleasant places to work. Under normal conditions, a court reporter can expect to work a standard

40 hours per week. During lengthy trials or other complicated proceedings, court reporters often work much longer hours. They must be on hand before and after the court is actually in session and must wait while a jury is deliberating. A court reporter often must be willing to work irregular hours, including some evenings. Court reporters must be able to spend long hours transcribing testimony with complete accuracy. There may be some travel involved, especially for freelance reporters and court reporters who are working for a traveling circuit judge. Normally, a court reporter will experience some down time without any transcript orders and then be hit all at once with several. This uneven workflow can cause the court reporter to have odd hours at times.

Court reporters spend time working with finances as well. Paperwork for record-keeping and tracking invoices, income, and expenses is part of the job.

Long hours of sitting in the same position can be tiring and court reporters may be bothered by eye and neck strain. There is also the risk of repetitive motion injuries, including carpal tunnel syndrome. The constant pressure to keep up and remain accurate can be stressful as well.

OUTLOOK

The U.S. Department of Labor predicts that employment of court reporters should grow much faster than the average for all occupations through 2016. Despite the rising number of criminal court cases and civil lawsuits, reduced budgets will limit employment opportunities for court reporters in local, state, and federal court systems. Job opportunities should be greatest in and around large metropolitan areas, but qualified court reporters should be able to find work in most parts of the country. There will be strong demand for court reporters who use their skills to produce captioning for live and taped television programs, which is a federal requirement for all television programming, and those who create real-time translations for the deaf and hard-of-hearing in legal and academic settings.

As always, job prospects will be best for those with the most training and experience. Because of the reliance on computers in many aspects of this job, computer experience and training are important. Court reporters who are certified—especially with the highest level of certification—will have the most opportunities to choose from.

As court reporters continue to use cutting-edge technology to make court transcripts more usable and accurate, the field itself should continue to grow.

FOR MORE INFORMATION

For information on digital/electronic court reporting and certification, contact

American Association of Electronic Reporters and Transcribers
23812 Rock Circle
Bothell, WA 98021-8573
Tel: 800-233-5306
Email: aaert@blarg.net
http://www.aaert.org

For information on certification and court reporting careers, contact

National Court Reporters Association
8224 Old Courthouse Road
Vienna, VA 22182-3808
Tel: 800-272-6272
Email: msic@ncrahq.org
http://www.ncraonline.org

For information on scholarships, contact

National Court Reporters Foundation
8224 Old Courthouse Road
Vienna, VA 22182-3808
Tel: 800-272-6272
Email: msic@ncrahq.org
http://ncraonline.org/Foundation

For tips on preparing for certification exams, and for career information, contact

National Verbatim Reporters Association
207 Third Avenue
Hattiesburg, MS 39401-3868
Tel: 601-582-4345
Email: nvra@aol.com
http://www.nvra.org

This organization represents court reporters who are employed at the federal level.

United States Court Reporters Association
4725 North Western Avenue, Suite 240
Chicago, IL 60625-2096
Tel: 800-628-2730
Email: uscra@uscra.org
http://www.uscra.org

Crime Analysts

OVERVIEW

Crime analysts analyze patterns in criminal behavior in order to catch criminals, predict patterns and motives of criminals, and improve the responsiveness of law enforcement agencies.

HISTORY

Crime has always been a major social problem, especially in heavily populated areas. Police and other law enforcement officials detect and apprehend criminals and protect citizens from robbery, violence, and other criminal acts. They are assisted by crime analysts—civilian workers who are hired to study crime statistics and patterns in order to give law enforcement officials an extra edge in fighting crime.

The earliest crime analysts simply analyzed raw crime statistics. Today, crime analysts use computer software, databases, and geographic information systems to predict and even prevent crimes. In recent years, crime analysis has become a popular career choice. This new technology and the emergence of community-oriented policing—which puts officers on the streets as opposed to behind a desk—have created many new opportunities for trained crime analysts.

THE JOB

Crime analysts try to uncover and piece together information about crime patterns, crime trends, and criminal suspects. It is a job that varies widely from day to day and from one state and law enforcement agency to the next. At its core is a systematic process that involves collecting, categorizing, analyzing, and sharing information in order to help the agency that a crime analyst works for better deploy officers on the street, work through difficult investigations, and increase arrests of criminals.

The basic work of a crime analyst involves collecting crime data from a range of sources, including police reports, statewide computer databases, crime newsletters, word-of-mouth tips, and interviews with suspects. To be useful, this information is then analyzed for patterns. Crime analysts are constantly vigilant for details that are similar or familiar. In addition to specific crime data, a crime analyst might study general factors such as population density, the demographic makeup of the population, commuting patterns, economic conditions (average income, poverty level, job availability), effectiveness of law enforcement agencies, citizens' attitudes toward crime, and crime reporting practices.

The responsibilities of crime analysts are often dependent upon the needs of their police department or law enforcement agency. One morning's tasks might include writing a profile on a particular demographic group's criminal patterns. On another day, an analyst could meet with the police chief to discuss an unusual string of local car thefts. Less frequently, the work includes going on "ride-alongs" with street cops, visiting a crime scene, or meeting with crime analysts from surrounding jurisdictions to exchange information about criminals who are plaguing the region. Occasionally, a crime analyst is pulled off of everyday responsibilities in order to work exclusively on a task force, usually focusing on a rash of violent crimes. As an ongoing responsibility, a crime analyst might be charged with tracking and monitoring "known offenders" (sex offenders, career criminals, repeat juvenile offenders, and parolees).

New computer technology has helped the crime analysis profession grow by leaps and bounds. In its earliest days, crime analysis simply meant gathering straight statistics on crime. Now these same statistics—coupled with specialized software—allow crime analysts to actually anticipate and prevent criminal activity.

The use of this analysis falls into three broad categories: *tactical*, *strategic*, and *administrative*. Tactical crime analysis aims at giving police officers and detectives prompt, in-the-field information that could lead to an arrest. These are the "hot" items that land on a crime analyst's desk, usually pertaining to specific crimes and offenders. For example, a criminal's mode of operation (M.O.) can be studied in order to predict who the likely next targets or victims will be. The police can then set up stakeouts or saturate the area with patrol cars. Tactical analysis is also used to do crime-suspect correlation, which involves identifying suspects for certain crimes based on their criminal histories.

Strategic analysis deals with finding solutions to long-range problems and crime trends. For instance, a crime analyst could create a crime trend forecast, based on current and past criminal activity, using computer software. An analyst might also perform a "manpower deployment" study to see if the police department is making the best use of its personnel. Another aspect of strategic analysis involves collating and disseminating demographic data on victims and geographic areas experiencing high crime rates so that the police are able to beef up crime prevention efforts.

Lastly, administrative analysis helps to provide policy-making information to a police department's administration. This might include a statistical study on the activity levels of police officers that would support a request for hiring more officers. Administrative work could also include creating graphs and charts that are used in management presentations or writing a speech on local crime prevention to give to the city council.

REQUIREMENTS

High School
While there are still a few law enforcement agencies that will hire crime analysts with only a high school diploma, it is becoming less common. Judy Kimminau, who works for the police department in Fort Collins, Colorado, says, "Crime analysis used to be a field that a person could stray into, but most new analysts now are trained or educated specifically for the career."

"While you're finishing up high school, it pays to hone your writing skills," Michelle Rankin, a former crime analyst, says. "You have to understand different styles of communicating so that you're able to write to the street cop and also to the city council." A good foundation in algebra will help with statistics classes in college. Moreover, take advantage of your school's computer lab, as basic knowledge of computers, word processing, spreadsheets, and databases is important.

Postsecondary Training
The majority of agencies require a bachelor's degree in criminal justice for the position of crime analyst. Excellent degrees to consider include statistics, computer science, and sociology.

A few colleges now offer undergraduate and graduate degrees and concentrations in crime analysis. These include the Indiana Institute of Technology (http://www.indianatech.edu), the University of New

Haven (http://www.newhaven.edu), St. Joseph's University (http://www.sju.edu), and Tiffin University (http://www.tiffin.edu).

Both Rankin and Kimminau agree that an internship during college is the best way to get a foot in the door and gain on-the-job experience. "Because of lean staffing, most units rely heavily on interns for support. The best thing is to contact a unit and talk with the crime analyst there," says Kimminau. She adds that a strong candidate for an internship would be organized, computer-literate, and have a basic understanding of statistics. In her unit, interns initially begin by reading police reports, learning how to glean significant facts and patterns from them. "It's pretty exciting the first time a spark goes off and an intern says, 'Hey, there's a pattern here!'"

Certification or Licensing

Currently, only California and Florida offer a formal, state-sponsored certification program for crime analysts. Individuals take 40 hours of courses on subjects such as crime analysis, criminal intelligence analysis, investigative analysis, and law enforcement research methods and statistics.

The International Association of Law Enforcement Intelligence Analysts also offers four levels of certification: basic, practitioner, advanced, and lifetime. The International Association of Crime Analysts offers the certified law enforcement analyst designation to applicants with three years of experience who pass an examination.

Other Requirements

Crime analysts need to be inquisitive, logical, and have a good memory for what they hear and read. A willingness to dig in and do this sort of research is also important, since much of the work involves piecing together disparate bits of information. Ask Steven Gottlieb, an internationally recognized crime analysis trainer, consultant, and executive director of the Alpha Group Center for Crime and Intelligence Analysis, just who will make a good crime analyst and he laughs, "Somebody who does crossword puzzles in ink." He explains that crime analysts love the process of working with bits of data that in and of themselves mean nothing. "It's only when you put them together that a clear picture emerges," he says.

Even though crime analysts are not out on the streets, they are immersed in the law enforcement milieu and come into contact with information that's potentially disturbing. "If a person becomes especially upset after reading reports on a murder or a child's molestation in the newspaper or after seeing a crime scene photo on television," notes Judy Kimminau, "they're probably not cut out for this line of work."

It is important to note that a crime analyst has to be willing to work in the background and not always be in the limelight. The positive side is that a crime analyst plays a significant role in all of the big cases, but does not have to wear a bulletproof vest in 100-degree heat or direct traffic in the rain.

EXPLORING

There are plenty of ways that you can begin your own training and education now. First of all, get some exposure to the law enforcement community by volunteering at the local police department. Many towns have a Boy Scouts Explorers program in which students (of both sexes) work to educate themselves about law enforcement.

EMPLOYERS

The majority of crime analysts are employed by local and state law enforcement agencies. A great number are also hired by federal agencies such as the Federal Bureau of Investigation (FBI), the Bureau of Customs and Border Protection, and the Department of Justice. In addition, some private security firms hire people with training in crime analysis.

STARTING OUT

While there is not a single, central clearinghouse for all crime analyst jobs, there are several places to look for listings. By becoming a member of the International Association of Crime Analysts (IACA), you will receive a newsletter that includes job openings. Judy Kimminau also advises finding out if there is a state association of crime analysts where you live and attend meetings, if possible. However, recent graduates would be best advised to be willing to move out of state if the job pickings are slim locally.

The key to getting a job in the field is doing an internship in college (see "Postsecondary Training"). In the past six months, Kimminau has assisted several agencies who are hiring crime analysts for the first time. "It's not unusual for recent college graduates to be hired, but all of these people had done internships." Michelle Rankin adds that a new crime analyst would have a solid shot at finding a job in a larger, established unit where he or she could volunteer first, learning from someone with greater experience.

Books to Read

Baker, Thomas E. *Introductory Criminal Analysis: Crime Prevention and Intervention Strategies.* Upper Saddle River, N.J.: Prentice Hall, 2004.

Barkan, Steven E. *Criminology: A Sociological Understanding.* 4th ed. Upper Saddle River, N.J.: Prentice Hall, 2008.

Boba, Rachel. *Crime Analysis and Crime Mapping.* Thousand Oaks, Calif.: Sage Publications, 2005.

Bruce, Christopher. *Exploring Crime Analysis: Readings on Essential Skills.* Charleston, S.C.: BookSurge Publishing, 2004.

Osborne, Deborah, and Susan Wernicke. *Introduction to Crime Analysis: Basic Resources for Criminal Justice Practice.* New York: Routledge, 2003.

Paulsen, Derek J., and Matt Robinson. *Crime Mapping and Spatial Analysis.* 2d ed. Boston: Allyn & Bacon, 2008.

Titus Reid, Sue. *Crime and Criminology.* 11th ed. New York: McGraw-Hill Humanities/Social Sciences/Languages, 2005.

ADVANCEMENT

As a broad generalization, most crime analysts are not pushing and shoving to climb the career ladder. Since theirs is often a one- or two-person, nonhierarchical unit within an agency, they more likely chose crime analysis because they relish the nature of the work itself. Obviously, advancement possibilities depend largely on the size and structure of the agency a crime analyst works for. In larger agencies, there are sometimes senior analysts, supervising analysts, or crime analysis managers. Some of these positions require a master's degree.

More often, crime analysts set their sights on increasing the impact they have on the agency and community in which they work.

Two careers that are closely linked to crime analysts are *criminal intelligence analyst* and *investigative analyst*. Criminal intelligence analysis involves the study of relationships between people, organizations, and events; it focuses on organized crime, money laundering, and other conspiratorial crimes. Investigative analysis attempts to uncover why a person is committing serial crimes such as murder and rape. Getting into the field of investigative analysis (sometimes called "profiling") usually requires years of experience and additional education in psychology—as well as good instincts.

EARNINGS

Earnings for crime analysts vary considerably, based on factors such as the location, the size of the employing agency and its financial status, and the analyst's experience. The IACA reports that salaries range from $35,000 to $65,000 or more per year.

Analysts receive the same benefits as others working in the same agency. These usually include paid vacation time, sick leave, health insurance, and retirement plans.

WORK ENVIRONMENT

The duties of crime analysts will vary based on the requirements of the law enforcement agency they work for. Analysts ordinarily work in the office analyzing crime information; occasionally, though, they may go on a "ride-along" with police officers or visit a crime scene to gather more information. Crime scenes can often be disturbing, and crime analysts need to act in a professional manner in these situations.

Analysts are constantly in communication with police chiefs, officers in the field, and fellow crime analysts as they work on a case. They need to establish good working relationships with officers who sometimes initially resent working with a civilian employee.

OUTLOOK

In the last five years, there has been a tremendous surge of interest in the field of crime analysis. One factor has been the emergence of community-oriented policing. This concept strives to get police officers out on the streets of their communities, rather than sitting at a desk. "With a limited number of officers, departments have to ask, 'What's the best use of their time?'" says Steven Gottlieb. "Good crime analysis helps to deploy officers in the right places at the right times."

Gottlieb believes that the future employment outlook for crime and intelligence analysts is very good. "Crime and intelligence analysts are now employed throughout all levels of government (federal, state, and municipal)," he says. "With the horrific events of 9/11 came an increasing realization that law enforcement needs specially trained people who can analyze the vast amounts of data gathered by officers and investigators and use it to create an accurate assessment of crime in their communities. As a result, law enforcement administrators are better able to police their jurisdictions on the basis of objective facts rather than mere perceptions."

The field is also growing because better software is becoming available. "When I started in the business," Gottlieb says, "all we had was a desk, a yellow pad, and good intentions. Today we have a formalized process for analyzing crime and the assistance of computers, automated information systems, mapping software, the Internet, and the ability to obtain information from our counterparts throughout the world at lightning speed. But all of the technology counts for nothing unless agencies have people who know how to use it to benefit their officers, investigators, administrators, and the citizens they serve. With their unique skills and abilities, crime and intelligence analysts are being hired with increasing frequency today."

While this growth trend is expected to continue, it's important to recognize that it is still a competitive job market. Those who want to become crime analysts should be willing to move to find an agency with a job opening. They should also bear in mind that police departments are historically more likely to lay off a civilian than a street officer.

FOR MORE INFORMATION

For information on careers in criminology, contact
American Society of Criminology
1314 Kinnear Road
Columbus, OH 43212-1156
Tel: 614-292-9207
http://www.asc41.com

For information on certification and membership, contact
International Association of Crime Analysts
9218 Metcalf Avenue, #364
Overland Park, KS 66212-1476
Tel: 800-609-3419
http://www.iaca.net

For information on certification, contact
International Association of Law Enforcement Intelligence Analysts
PO Box 13857
Richmond, VA 23225-8857
http://www.ialeia.org

Elder Law Attorneys

QUICK FACTS

School Subjects
English
Economics
Government

Personal Skills
Communication/
  ideas
Leadership/
  management

Work Environment
Primarily indoors
Primarily multiple locations

Minimum Education Level
Law degree

Salary Range
$50,580 to $102,470 to
$1,000,000+

Certification or Licensing
Voluntary (certification)
Required by all states
  (licensing)

Outlook
About as fast as the average

DOT
110

GOE
04.02.01

NOC
4112

O*NET-SOC
23-1011.00

OVERVIEW

Lawyers, or *attorneys,* work in our legal system as advocates and advisers. As advocates, they represent the rights of their clients in trials and depositions or in front of administrative and government bodies. As advisers, attorneys counsel clients on how the law affects business or personal decisions, such as the purchase of property or the creation of a will. Lawyers can represent individuals, businesses, and corporations. *Elder law attorneys* are lawyers who specialize in providing legal services for the elderly and, in some cases, the disabled. Unlike other lawyers who deal with one field of law, such as tax lawyers, elder law attorneys often deal with several fields of law when providing services to their clients. Some of the most common elder law issues include guardianship or conservatorship, public benefits (Medicaid, Medicare, and Social Security), probate and estate planning, health and long-term care planning, and elder abuse cases. The National Academy of Elder Law Attorneys (NAELA) reports that its current membership is 5,000. In addition, there are thousands of attorneys who practice elder law as a part of a law practice that encompasses a range of other areas.

HISTORY

Over the centuries, societies have built up systems of law that have been studied and drawn upon by later governments. The earliest known law is the Code of Hammurabi, developed about 1800 B.C. by the ruler of the Sumerians. Another early set of laws was the law of Moses, also known as the Ten Commandments. Every set of laws, no matter when it was introduced, has been accompanied by the need for someone to explain those laws and help others live under them.

Much modern European law was organized and refined by legal experts assembled by Napoleon; their body of law was known as the Napoleonic Code. English colonists coming to America brought English common law, which influenced the development of much of American law. As the population in the country grew and the number of businesses increased, those who knew the law were in high demand. The two main kinds of law are civil and criminal, but many other specialty areas are also prevalent today. When the United States was a young country, most lawyers were general law practitioners; they knew and worked with all the laws for their clients. Today, as laws have grown more complex, an increasing number of lawyers specialize and limit their practices to certain areas, such as tax law, corporate law, and intellectual property law.

In the 20th century, the number of Americans over the age of 65 increased dramatically. One significant reason for this increase was medical and technological advances that extended life spans. As the older population became larger, its members began to experience problems and have concerns that affected all of society, including financing the post-retirement years, the increased need for nursing homes and medical/geriatric care, the legal and ethical issues regarding the care of individuals with diminished capabilities, and the frequent difficulty of getting the appropriate public benefits. Senior citizens who may never have seen an attorney in their lives can find themselves in need of legal advice and advocacy. Out of necessity, elder law has developed to meet their needs. In addition, one of the largest generations in our country's history—the "baby boomers" who were born between 1945 and 1965—will soon become a part of this older generation (approximately from the early 2010s to the 2030s). As this large generation ages, the demand for elder law attorneys should increase.

THE JOB

Lawyers can give legal advice and, when necessary, represent their clients' interests in court. Regardless of their area of expertise, an attorney's job is to help clients know and understand their legal rights and to help them assert those rights before a judge, jury, government agency, or other legal forum, such as an arbitration panel.

Elder law attorneys focus on the needs of their elderly clients, using a variety of legal tools and techniques to meet their goals in an efficient, fiscally responsible, and legally sound manner. Elder law attorneys deal with the whole of the legal needs of their clients. Because of this, their responsibilities are many. They may help one client with estate planning; they may counsel another client about planning for mental incapacity and compose an alternative decision-making document that will allow another family member, for example, to make decisions about that client's health care; and they may assist yet another client in planning for possible long-term care needs, including nursing home care. Locating the appropriate type of care, coordinating private and public resources to finance the cost of care, and working to ensure the client's right to quality care are all part of the elder law practice.

Elder law lawyers must know the law's position on a variety of issues, including health and long-term care planning, surrogate decision-making (that is, when the client has appointed someone, most likely a relative, to make financial or other decisions when the client is unable to), obtaining public benefits (including Medicaid, Medicare, and Social Security), managing diminished capacity (such as when the client can no longer think clearly), and the conservation and administration of the older person's estate (including wills, trusts, and probate). In advising about these matters, elder law attorneys must know about the tax consequences for clients when they decide on a certain action (such as putting money in a trust). Attorneys must also recognize when they need to seek out more sophisticated tax information from an expert and do so for the best interests of their clients. In addition, elder law attorneys must be able to recognize cases of abuse, neglect, and exploitation of an older client. An elder law attorney must also be familiar with professional and non-legal resources and services that are publicly and privately available to meet the needs of the older person. Elder law lawyers can then refer clients to these resources, which may include adult day care centers, community transportation, and food services. Elder law encompasses more than just legal planning; it deals with a larger realm of life planning.

In many cases, a crisis is what brings a new client to an elder law attorney. Common situations include middle-income families concerned about paying for a parent's long-term care and nursing home care; families with an older member whose ability to think clearly and live independently is diminishing; older people wanting to ensure their wishes are respected when their health deteriorates; families struggling with retirement and/or assisted-living decisions, contracts, and expenses; and families or seniors faced with issues of age discrimination, exploitation, or abuse.

Elder law attorneys must conduct their practices ethically. They must understand their clients, know which confidences can be shared with which family members, and know when and how to seek other professionals, whether about medical, financial, insurance, or tax issues, to best meet the needs of the clients. The attorney must also recognize situations where a client's wishes clash with those of the family and then determine the best way of handling the issues to best serve the client.

REQUIREMENTS

High School

To become a lawyer you will need to get a college degree and a law degree after you graduate from high school. To start preparing for this later education and career, take a college preparatory curriculum, including math, science, and a foreign language, while in high school. Be sure to take courses in social studies, government, history, and economics to prepare for law studies. English courses are also important for building your writing, researching, and speaking skills. And because lawyers often use technology to research and interpret the law, take advantage of any computer-related classes or experience you can get. Even surfing the Internet can provide experience in doing research online.

Postsecondary Training

To enter any law school approved by the American Bar Association, you must satisfactorily complete at least three, and usually four, years of college work. Most law schools do not specify any particular courses for prelaw education. The traditional majors for college students intending to pursue a postgraduate law degree are history, English, philosophy, political science, economics, and business. Other successful law students have focused their undergraduate studies in areas as diverse as art, music theory, computer science, engineering, nursing, and education. A college student planning to specialize in elder law might also take courses significantly related to that area, such as social sciences, psychology, economics, and courses related to health care.

To gain admission to law school, most programs require applicants to take the Law School Admission Test (LSAT). The LSAT tests students on analytical thinking, writing, and problem-solving skills. Most full-time law degree programs take three years to complete. There are currently 195 approved law schools in the United States. State authorities approve additional programs, many of them part-time or night school programs that can be completed in four years. You should contact law schools you are interested in to find out specific requirements for their programs. College guidance counselors and professors may also be valuable sources of information.

The first year of typical law school programs consists of required courses, such as legal writing and research, contracts, criminal law, constitutional law, torts, and property. First-year law students are required to read and study thousands of legal cases. The second and third years are usually focused on specialized courses of interest to the student. In the case of elder law, students might take course work in public policy, health law, medical ethics, and geriatrics.

Upon completing law school, students usually receive the yuris doctor (JD) degree or bachelor of laws (LLB) degree.

Certification or Licensing

To obtain a law license, lawyers (regardless of their specialization) must be admitted to the bar association of the state in which they will practice. Bar admission standards in most states require that students graduate from an approved law school and that they pass a bar examination in the state in which they intend to practice. These exams, usually lasting two days, have questions about various areas of the law, such as constitutional law and criminal law. The tests may also include an essay section and a professional responsibility section. It is important to note, however, that each state sets its own standards for taking the bar exam, and a few states allow exceptions to the educational requirements. For example, a small number of states allow a person who has spent several years reading law in a law office and has some law school experience to take the state bar exam. A few states allow people who have completed law study through correspondence programs to take the bar. In addition, some states require that newly graduated lawyers serve a period of clerkship in an established law firm before they are eligible to take the bar examination. Because of such variations, you will need to contact the bar examiners board of your state for specific information on its requirements.

Specialized voluntary certification is available for elder law attorneys. The National Elder Law Foundation (NELF) offers certification to attorneys who have been in practice five years or longer, have spent at least 16 hours per week (over three years) practicing elder law, have handled at least 60 elder law matters, and have had at least 45 hours of continuing legal education in elder law. To obtain certification, applicants must also pass an examination. After five years, certified attorneys must be recertified to maintain their status.

Other Requirements

All lawyers have to be effective communicators, work well with people, and be able to find creative solutions to problems, such as complex court cases. Elder lawyers, however, need to have some special skills and personality characteristics. They need to understand how aging affects the mind and body, how conflicts can arise among family members regarding the best interests of an elderly member, and how the family's wishes sometimes are in conflict with those of the older person. This work requires perceptiveness, ethics, and diplomacy. Barbara Fox, an attorney practicing elder law at Ray, Fleischer, and Fox in Chicago, asserts that listening to and truly understanding a client is one of the most important skills for an elder law attorney. "People come in with family members who may have differing concerns and opinions, but you need to focus on the wants and needs of your client. It's important always to remember who your client is."

EXPLORING

You can explore this profession by finding out more about being a lawyer and by gaining experience working with the elderly. To learn more about the legal profession in general, sit in on some trials at your local or state courthouse. Watch the lawyers and take note of what they do. Write down questions you have and terms or actions you don't understand so you can research them later. Work with your guidance counselor to set up an information interview with a lawyer willing to answer questions about the career. You may also be able to "job shadow" this person for part of a workday or more. By doing this, you can see some of the typical daily work of a lawyer. You may even be able to help with some tasks, such as filing.

An elder law attorney consults with a client. (*Jeff Greenberg, The Image Works*)

The Internet is also a good source of information. You can go to law-related sites to learn more about legal terminology, current court cases, and the field of law in general. Some sites that would be particularly beneficial to visit include those of the American Bar Association, NAELA, and NELF. (See the end of this article for their Web addresses.) You can also try to get part-time or summer work in a lawyer's office. You may only answer phones, file office papers, or type letters, but this work will give you excellent exposure to the profession.

It will also be important for you to get experience working with the elderly, either on a paid or a volunteer basis. Contact local nursing homes, senior centers, and volunteer groups providing services, such as Meals on Wheels, to find out what opportunities are available. By working with the elderly population, you will start to learn about their specific needs, concerns, and opinions.

EMPLOYERS

The majority of practicing elder law attorneys in the United States work in private practice, either in law firms or alone. While it may seem that the best employment possibilities might be found in large cities and metropolitan areas, there is also fierce competition in these places. Many attorneys practice elder law in addition to other areas of law. Additionally, clients often come to their regular attorneys for elder issues that arise in their lives. Since elder law is so client-oriented, the logical approach is to practice where there is a large population of elderly people; therefore, smaller, more rural areas offer numerous opportunities. In addition, the cost of living is lower in these areas, and since the majority of people seeking elder law attorneys are not wealthy and cannot pay astronomical fees, the elder law attorney will find living on a typical income easier in these areas.

STARTING OUT

After graduation from law school, a lawyer's first task is to pass the state bar examination. A new lawyer will often find a job with a law firm, doing research for other lawyers until passing the bar examination and becoming licensed to practice law. Beginning lawyers usually do not go into solo practice right away. It is difficult to become established, and the experience of working beside established lawyers is helpful to the fledgling lawyer. Newly admitted lawyers typically do research and routine work at first. Specialization usually occurs after a lawyer has some experience in general practice, although lawyers at smaller firms might find themselves guided to particular areas earlier. After a few years of successful experience, a lawyer may be ready to go out on his or her own.

Many new lawyers are recruited directly from law school by law firms or other employers. Recruiters come to the law school and interview possible hires. Recent graduates can also get job leads from local and state bar associations.

To start building a practice in elder law, take as many cases that fall into the realm of elder law as you can and become a member of the NAELA. When you have enough experience under your belt and meet the necessary qualifications, become certified as an elder law attorney with the NELF.

ADVANCEMENT

Lawyers with outstanding ability may expect to go a long way in their profession. Beginning lawyers generally start out doing routine research tasks, but as they prove themselves and develop their abilities, opportunities for advancement will arise. They may be promoted to junior partner in a law firm or establish their own practice focused on elder law.

Advancement for elder law attorneys can also take the form of leadership positions in nonprofit organizations that serve to advance education and competence in the field. There are many opportunities to make a contribution to the elderly population by working to support or change the laws and policies that affect senior citizens. In this unique area of legal practice, the potential for reward, although usually not as financially large as other areas of the law, is great.

EARNINGS

Beginning lawyers earn a modest salary, but the potential for higher earnings builds quickly with solid experience. A lawyer just starting out in solo practice may barely make ends meet for the first few years, especially since many law-school graduates carry $70,000–$80,000 in student loan debt. According to the U.S. Department of Labor, the 2006 median salary for practicing lawyers was $102,470, although some senior partners earned well over $1 million a year. Ten percent earned less than $50,580. General attorneys in the federal government received $116,700 in 2006. State and local government attorneys generally made less, earning $77,970 and $84,570, respectively, in 2006.

According to the National Association for Law Placement, median salaries for new lawyers employed seven months after graduation were $60,000 in 2005. Those working for the government made approximately $46,158. Starting salaries for lawyers in business were $60,000. Recent graduates entering private practice made the most, earning approximately $85,000. Although salaries for private practice law are attractive, it is important to remember that lawyers just starting out may barely make ends meet for the first few years. Most law-school graduates carry upwards of $70,000 in student loans. Thus, although many graduates may want to work in public service and government law, many take jobs in private practice in order to gain a stronger financial foothold.

Incomes for elder law attorneys vary greatly but generally are less than those of their colleagues working with wealthy clients, such as corporate lawyers representing major companies.

Benefits and bonuses vary widely in this field. Many attorneys are sole practitioners and therefore don't receive company benefits such as paid vacation, health insurance, and retirement plans. Generally, lawyers who are partners in larger firms may enjoy more generous benefits packages and perks than those with a sole practice.

WORK ENVIRONMENT

Lawyers typically enjoy a pleasant, although busy, work environment. Law offices are usually designed to impress clients and can be quite comfortable. Lawyers may also spend significant time in law libraries or record rooms or in the homes and offices of clients. Courtrooms are usually orderly and efficient workplaces. However, many elder law lawyers never work in a courtroom, and, unless directly involved in litigation, they may never work at a trial.

Working hours for most lawyers are usually regular business hours. Many lawyers, however, have to work long hours when a client's case demands it, spending evenings and weekends preparing cases and materials and working with clients. Besides the time spent working directly on a client's needs, lawyers must always keep up with the latest developments in the profession. Lawyers who work in law firms must often work long hours for senior partners in order to advance in the firm. Spending long weekend hours doing research and interviewing people should be expected.

Elder law attorneys, more than other types of lawyers, can expect to put in more hours visiting their clients in their homes or care facilities, since traveling to the attorney's office may be challenging for some clients. Attorneys who specialize in elder law should be prepared for the realities of life for the elderly, as they are likely to be exposed to various types and stages of illness or infirmity and environments that can be disturbing to some.

OUTLOOK

According to the U.S. Department of Labor, the demand for all lawyers is expected to grow as fast as the average for all occupations through 2016, but those in the specialty of elder law will have the advantage of a rapidly growing elderly population, increasingly complex laws, and unprecedented health care issues. All of these factors combine to make for a substantial client base in need of elder law attorneys. It is estimated that 40 percent of people over 65 will require a nursing home or other long-term care at some point, but few of them have planned financially for that eventuality. People are living longer and encountering a variety of health care problems, many of them debilitating. The sheer numbers of elderly people alone point to a promising future in this career.

However, the outlook is also affected by governmental changes and public policy. Barbara Fox points out that since a majority of elder law clients are seeking legal advice and assistance for Medicare/Medicaid issues, the outlook for the profession is significantly affected by changes in law. If there is a decrease in public benefits, this will affect the workload for elder law attorneys. She also advises that many people do not seek out an elder law attorney in particular for issues such as long-range planning, asset protection, guardianship, and probate practices; rather, they are likely to bring these issues to their regular attorney. In other words, attorneys who may not specialize in elder law often handle a large number of cases involving elder law issues.

The large number of law school graduates each year has created strong competition for jobs, and new attorneys, even those with an eye toward elder law specialization, will initially face stiff competition for jobs.

Lawyers in solo practice will find it hard to earn a living until their practice and reputation are fully established. The best opportunities exist in small towns or suburbs of large cities, where there is less competition and new lawyers can meet potential clients more easily.

FOR MORE INFORMATION

For information about law student services, approved law schools, and the ABA Commission on Legal Problems of the Elderly, contact
American Bar Association (ABA)
321 North Clark Street
Chicago, IL 60610-4714
Tel: 800-285-2221
Email: askaba@abanet.org
http://www.abanet.org and http://www.abanet.org/aging

For information on AALS members, contact
Association of American Law Schools (AALS)
1201 Connecticut Avenue, NW, Suite 800
Washington, DC 20036-2717
Tel: 202-296-8851
Email: aals@aals.org
http://www.aals.org

For information on elder law, contact
National Academy of Elder Law Attorneys
1604 North Country Club Road
Tucson, AZ 85716-3119
Tel: 520-881-4005
http://www.naela.org

For information about certification in elder law, contact
National Elder Law Foundation
1604 North Country Club Road
Tucson, AZ 85716-3119
Tel: 520-881-1076
http://www.nelf.org

For more information on issues affecting the elderly, contact the
following organizations:
National Institute on Aging
Building 31, Room 5C27
31 Center Drive, MSC 2292
Bethesda, MD 20892-0001
Tel: 301-496-1752
http://www.nia.nih.gov

U.S. Administration on Aging
330 Independence Avenue, SW
Washington, DC 20201-0003
Tel: 202-619-0724
Email: aoainfo@aoa.hhs.gov
http://www.aoa.dhhs.gov

INTERVIEW

Victoria Heuler is a board certified elder law attorney at Mcconnaughhay, Duffy, Coonrod, Pope & Weaver, P.A. in Tallahassee, Florida. She is also the president of the Academy of Florida Elder

Law Attorneys. Victoria discussed her career with the editors of Careers in Focus: Law.

Q. Why did you decide to become an elder law attorney?

A. I decided to become an elder law attorney because I wanted to practice in an area of law that was personally gratifying. It was important to me to know that I was helping someone every single day of my life. With elder law, the confirmation of helping people does really come every day and sometimes many times in one day. Instead of wondering over the course of a year if I am making a difference, I get immediate gratification that what I do helps individuals, their families, and other loved ones. I also wanted to be able to give of my natural talents. It is easy for me to want to help people, to be compassionate toward their plight, to want to listen to their issues and concerns, and to want to help our aging friends have the best life they can before they pass on from this earth. It is easy to get out of bed each morning knowing that I can have this kind of impact on my clients.

Q. What were your expectations entering this field? Are they much different from the realities?

A. I expected in entering the area of elder law that I would be working directly with persons who were in their elder years and helping make sure their needs were protected. I also expected that the practice would be virtually all "warm and fuzzy" in terms of everyone wanting to help the older person achieve the best life possible. Additionally, I thought I would give and they would receive.

Some of the realities of being an elder law attorney *are* different than I expected. For example, I have learned that not all persons have the same view of what is necessary to protect an older person. Some—often family members—believe that an elder is best served by another person making all of that elder's decisions, regardless of whether the elder is capable of making his or her own decisions. This is what is called *paternalistic* behavior and is a viewpoint that suggests ageism—that as we age, we are presumptively less capable of handling our own affairs. I disagree with this view. That warm and fuzzy world I expected is not always the reality, with litigation being more prominent in my practice than I thought it would be. Litigation in elder law will increase as our population ages.

The practice is also more fast-paced than I expected because we are dealing with individual lives and problems as they occur, which can mean several emergencies in a day requiring rapid decision-making and advice.

I love the fact that I am given so much by my clients and their families, most of whom are truly wonderful people and really trying to do right by each other. I learn so much from my older clients and was not expecting to be so enriched by them when I entered the area of elder law. It is one of those intangible benefits of the practice that makes this area so special.

Q. Take us through a day in your life as an elder law attorney. What are your typical tasks/responsibilities?

A. I usually arrive at the office around 9:00 A.M. and work through lunch most days. The first thing I do is check my voice messages to determine if any "fires" (i.e., emergencies) have to be put out first thing before my day proceeds. If such a fire exists, my elder law team (one paralegal and one legal assistant) works with me to handle the issues while we get ready for the rest of the day.

I usually meet with, talk to, or email correspond with several clients each day. Today, I met with a guardian whose ward (the person in whose shoes the guardian stands) had recently died. During the meeting, we discussed issues ranging from funeral arrangements, notification to family, how to close the guardianship post-death, whether a challenge to decedent's will would ensue, and the current and ongoing familial relationships. My responsibilities in that case were to guide the guardian in understanding his duty to finally account for the ward's property, report to the court, and turn the remaining assets over to the likely estate representative. After my initial client appointment, I checked my numerous emails and replied to some.

I am the president of the Academy of Florida Elder Law Attorneys, so I have additional responsibilities and necessary communications this year.

I also received and responded to a few client emails, which are encouraged for efficiency. I then met with the second client, who showed up unexpectedly, but for whom we needed to resolve some issues (it is not that unusual for a client to just "show up" and for us to be gracious and do what we can to help the person). My legal assistant and I met with the client and discussed some questions that had arisen regarding her sibling's behavior and the effect on the guardianship for their mother. I provided emotional support and guided her through the laws and rules regarding guardianships in helping her carry out her responsibilities as guardian. I also helped create a working solution for a particular problem that may avoid litigation. I am frequently called upon to interpret the laws as they apply to particular cases, and to play out scenarios for clients regarding a course of action they may want to take. Client actions may be "legal," but might not make sense when I help them play out the possible ramifications in terms of the older person or the larger family unit.

Q. What is your work environment like? Do you travel for your job?

A. My work environment is very nice. I work within a larger law firm, McConnaughhay, Duffy, Coonrod, Pope & Waver, P.A., in Tallahassee, Florida, and our firm handles worker's compensation and general civil litigation, as well as elder law, probate, and appeals. Many elder law attorneys are actually sole practitioners where they are the only attorney in their office and have several staff members working with them.

I work on the lower floor of a two-story building—the lower floor being helpful for older people, but we also have an elevator if we need to use an upstairs conference room. You do have to think about accommodations when in an elder law practice! Parking and building access are very convenient to our clients, which is incredibly important for a positive lawyer/client experience.

In terms of "work environment," I would also include my elder law peers as a positive part of the working environment. Most elder law attorneys are incredibly compassionate and giving to other elder law attorneys, as well as their own clients! Attorneys in other practice areas are not often heard saying this of their own practice areas. We in elder law are blessed to have a very collegial bar.

I do travel for my job sometimes. I will travel to a client's home to visit with him or her, or to the assisted living facility or nursing home, if that is required or requested. I also travel out of town if I have a court matter in another county, sometimes driving as far as four hours. Travel involving flights is rare, although this can occur if I am involved in litigation and need to take a deposition of a person living far enough away.

Q. What do you like most and least about your job?

A. I am a very positive person and I believe in the ability of people to do the right thing, particularly if given the right tools with which to work. Therefore, I particularly like that my job allows me to help clients and their families problem-solve toward a better existence. I help clients better understand their legal rights; I help them put their wishes into a legal document to better communicate their wishes to family and others; and I assist clients in developing the least intrusive means of helping their loved one so dignity and autonomy can be preserved.

My least favorite part of what I do as an elder law attorney is seeing families battling each other, often over or about a parent. It can be incredibly sad to witness family members' viciousness toward each other, made even sadder knowing that they will be left with only their hate for each other once their parent or parents are gone.

Q. What advice would you give to young people who are interested in this career?

A. My advice is to talk to your family members, starting with your elders, and listen to their stories. It is eye-opening and fascinating to hear the lives that many of our elders have led. I also encourage young people to read about the lives of older people and some of the issues that older people face in our country and around the world. There are many issues yet to be successfully handled regarding the larger population of older people that will inhabit our planet in the next several decades. Get to know the subject matter. Elder law requires general knowledge in a lot of areas of law, as well as general knowledge in matters of social work, gerontology, medicine, and behavior. Take some courses in gerontology, sociology, or psychology in college to get a broad understanding of some of the dynamics that will present themselves in a career where elders are the focus. Finally, be ready to work hard, but feel great about what you can do for other people. It is truly a fascinating and invigorating practice area!

Forensic Accountants and Auditors

OVERVIEW

Forensic accountants and auditors, sometimes known as *investigative accountants, investigative auditors,* and *certified fraud examiners,* use accounting principles and theories to support or oppose claims being made in litigation. Like other accountants and auditors, forensic accountants are trained to analyze and verify financial records. However, forensic accountants use these skills to identify and document financial wrongdoing. They prepare reports that may be used in criminal and civil trials. The word "forensic" means "suitable for a court of law, public debate, or formal argumentation." There are approximately 1.3 million accountants and auditors, a category that includes forensic accountants and auditors, employed in the United States.

HISTORY

People have used accounting and bookkeeping procedures for as long as they have engaged in trade. Records of accounts have been preserved from ancient and medieval times.

Modern bookkeeping dates back to the advent of double-entry bookkeeping, a method of tracking the impact of transactions on both a company's assets and profitability. Double-entry bookkeeping was developed in medieval Italy. The earliest known published work about this system was written in 1494 by an Italian monk named Luca Pacioli. Pacioli did not invent the system, but he did summarize principles that remain largely unchanged today.

Records preserved from 16th century Europe indicate that formulations were developed during that time to account for assets, liabilities, and income. When the industrial revolution swept through the world in the 18th century, accounting became even more sophisticated to accommodate the acceleration of financial transactions caused by mechanization and mass production.

In the 20th and 21st centuries, accounting has become a more creative and interesting discipline. Computers now perform many routine computations, while accountants tend to spend more time interpreting the results. Many accountants now hold senior management positions within large organizations. They assess the possible impact of various transactions, mergers, and acquisitions and help companies manage their employees more efficiently.

While people have probably investigated financial records for as long as people have kept accounts, forensic accounting did not emerge as a distinct area of specialty until quite recently. The increased litigation and white-collar crime that emerged in the 1980s (and continues today) has contributed to rapid growth in this field.

THE JOB

Forensic accountants and auditors have all the skills that traditional accountants and auditors possess. They are trained to compile, verify, and analyze financial records and taxes. They monitor the efficiency of business procedures and management. Unlike traditional accountants, however, forensic accountants use their skills to help clients prepare for trials.

"Forensic accounting," says Jim DiGabriele, of DiGabriele, McNulty & Co., "uses investigative skills to follow paper trails. We follow financial documents to the end of the trail and then we more or less prepare reports for litigation."

In an investigation, the forensic accountant usually begins by reviewing relevant financial and business documents and interviewing the people involved. He or she also may assemble relevant third-party information, such as economic data for comparable industries or companies. Using the compiled information, the forensic accountant may then calculate the losses or damages caused by any financial violations or errors. Finally, the forensic accountant prepares a detailed report explaining his or her findings and conclusions. This report is intended for use in litigation.

"Only about one in 20 cases actually goes to litigation," notes Tom Fox, a forensic accountant with Davidson, Fox & Co., "but a forensic accountant must treat each and every report as if it is going to trial. Forensic accountants must carefully document and date every related conversation and scrap of information."

If a case is scheduled to proceed to litigation, the attorneys involved may schedule a deposition. A deposition is a pretrial hearing, in which attorneys from both sides may interview one another's witnesses to gain information about the case. Forensic accountants sometimes help attorneys prepare questions for these depositions. They also are sometimes asked to answer questions in a deposition.

If and when a case finally goes to trial, a forensic accountant also may serve as an expert witness and testify before the court. Forensic accountants may offer testimony regarding the nature of the violation, a person's or company's guilt or innocence, and the amount of the resulting damages. As expert witnesses, forensic accountants must be able to present information in a clear and organized manner. They must be able to explain complicated accounting concepts in a way that can be understood by people who are not in the field. They must be able to explain and defend the methods they used to arrive at their conclusions.

There is no "typical" case for a forensic accountant. Forensic accountants use their skills to investigate a wide variety of situations or violations.

Many insurance companies hire forensic accountants to evaluate claims they suspect may be inflated or fraudulent. If an insured company files a claim for a business interruption loss, for example, the insurance company may hire a forensic accountant to ensure that the company's loss was as great as the company claims it was. To make this assessment, the forensic accountant must review the company's past financial records. Before calculating the company's probable loss, the forensic accountant also must consider the current marketplace. If the economy is booming and the market for the company's products or services is hot, the insured's losses may be substantial. If the economy is sluggish, or if the company's product has become obsolete, the losses may be much lower.

Insurance companies also hire forensic accountants to assess claimants' loss of income due to accidents or disability, or property loss to fire, flood, or theft. Occasionally, a claimant may hire a forensic accountant to defend his or her claim or to rebut another forensic accountant's testimony.

Forensic accountants also investigate malpractice claims against accountants or auditors. In these cases, forensic accountants must examine the reports prepared by the accountants and auditors to determine whether they followed accepted procedures. If the forensic accountant does discover an error, he or she also may be required to calculate the financial impact of the discrepancy.

Companies sometimes hire forensic accountants to determine whether employees are taking bribes from vendors or customers in return for offering higher payments or lower prices. Companies also hire forensic accountants to detect insider trading. Insider trading occurs when an employee uses privileged information to make a profit—or helps someone else make a profit—by buying or selling stock. Forensic accountants also assist corporate clients by calculating loss due to breach of contract, patent infringement, and fraud.

Some forensic accountants engage in divorce valuation work. These professionals determine the value of the personal assets, liabilities, pensions, and business holdings of individuals involved in a divorce settlement.

REQUIREMENTS

High School

If you are interested in entering this field, take as many math and computer classes as possible in high school. You also should take any available business classes, because forensic accountants must understand basic business procedures in order to assess business interruption losses. Forensic accountants who eventually form their own accounting firms also will need management and administrative skills. Business classes can provide you with a solid foundation in these areas.

Writing, speech, and communication classes are extremely useful courses to take. A forensic accountant's value to clients depends entirely on his or her ability to provide credible reports and convincing testimony for trial. For this reason, forensic accountants must be able to write clear, organized reports. They must be able to speak clearly and audibly in courtrooms. They must appear poised and confident when speaking publicly, and they must be able to convey complicated information in comprehensible language.

Postsecondary Training

Once in college, you should major in accounting or major in business administration with a minor in accounting. "Mind you," says Tom Fox, "you don't get out of college as a forensic accountant. You get out of college ready to be an accountant and then you learn forensic techniques through experience." Also included in your course of study should be computer classes, as well as English or communication classes. In the past several years, a few colleges (such as Carlow University, Franklin University, Mount Marty College, Myers University, and Waynesburg College) have started offering degrees and concentrations in forensic accounting, but most students still prepare for this field by majoring in accounting and learning forensic accounting techniques on the job.

Some organizations prefer to hire accountants with master's degrees in accounting or master's in business administration. So, depending on what company you want to work for, you may need to continue your education beyond the college level.

Certification or Licensing

Anyone who is interested in becoming a forensic accountant should first become a certified public accountant (CPA). While it is theoretically possible to practice as a forensic accountant without becoming a CPA, it is extremely unlikely that anyone would succeed in so doing. Clients hire forensic accountants with the idea that they may eventually serve as expert witnesses. A forensic accountant who is not certified could be easily discredited in a trial.

To become a CPA, most states require candidates to have completed 150 credit hours, or the equivalent of a master's degree, in an accounting program of study. The American Institute of Certified Public Accountants (AICPA) is working to make this a national standard for accounting education as accounting procedures and reporting laws become increasingly more complex. Candidates for the credential also must pass the Uniform CPA Examination, which is developed by the AICPA. Finally, many states require candidates to have a certain amount of professional experience (usually at least two years) to qualify for certification. Most states also require CPAs to earn about 40 hours of continuing education each year.

AICPA members who have valid CPA certificates may also earn the following specialty designations: accredited in business valuation, certified information technology professional, and personal financial specialist.

A CPA who has gained some experience should consider becoming a certified fraud examiner (CFE). Forensic accountants and fraud examiners use many of the same skills. In fact, the titles are sometimes used interchangeably, although, according to the National Association of Forensic Accountants (NAFA), fraud examiners are more often concerned with developing procedures and implementing measures to prevent fraud. However, the two areas are not mutually exclusive; many forensic accountants also work as fraud examiners and vice versa. To gain the CFE designation, a CPA must meet certain educational and professional experience requirements and pass the Uniform CFE Examination, which is administered by the Association of Certified Fraud Examiners. The designation can help forensic accountants establish their credibility as expert witnesses. CFEs must complete a certain amount of continuing education each year.

The National Association of Forensic Accountants also offers certification to its members. Contact the association for more information.

Other Requirements

Forensic accountants are the sleuths of the financial world. Consequently, they must be curious and dogged in their pursuit of answers. They must have exceptional attention to detail and be capable of intense concentration. Like every professional involved with the judicial system, forensic accountants and auditors are frequently subject to abrupt schedule changes, so they also should be able to work under stressful conditions and meet exceptionally tight deadlines. They also must have excellent communication skills and they must be poised and confident.

EXPLORING

Opportunities for high school students to explore this field are limited. You may, however, contact people in this field to request information interviews. Information interviews can be an excellent way to learn about different careers.

Hone your math skills outside of the classroom by joining your high school math team or by volunteering as a math tutor at your school or a local learning center. You can also improve you business and accounting skills by joining a school group that has a yearly budget and offering to be the treasurer. This will give you the opportunity to be responsible for an organization's financial records.

Try landing a summer job performing clerical tasks for accounting or law firms. This experience can help you become familiar with the documentation necessary in both fields. When in college, you should seek internship positions with accounting firms in order to gain practical experience and to make contacts within the industry.

EMPLOYERS

Approximately 1.3 million accountants and auditors (a category that includes forensic accountants and auditors) are employed in the United States. Forensic accountants and auditors usually work for accounting companies that provide litigation support for insurance companies, law firms, and other parties involved in litigation.

STARTING OUT

Most people spend several years working as accountants before specializing in forensic accounting. Their first hurdle after college is to find employment as an accountant. College professors and career placement counselors can help accounting majors arrange interviews with respected accounting firms and government agencies. Students also can contact these firms and agencies directly to learn about job opportunities. Many accounting firms and government positions are advertised in newspapers and on the Internet.

In general, accounting firms tend to offer better starting salaries than government agencies. Larger firms also sometimes have entire departments dedicated to litigation support services. New graduates who secure positions with these firms might have opportunities to learn the forensic ropes while gaining experience as accountants. With time, after earning a CPA and gaining experience, an accountant within a large firm may have an opportunity to specialize in litigation support and forensic accounting. The largest firms include PricewaterhouseCoopers, Ernst & Young, Deloitte Touche Tohmatsu, and KPMG International.

Another excellent way to gain relevant experience is by working for the Internal Revenue Service (IRS). IRS auditors and accountants use many of the same skills necessary for forensic accountants. Jim DiGabriele and his partner both worked as IRS auditors before leaving to form their own forensic accounting firm.

ADVANCEMENT

Forensic accountants usually advance by gaining experience and establishing reputations for integrity, thorough documentation, and reliable calculations. As a forensic accountant gains experience, he or she usually attracts more clients and is able to work on more interesting, complex cases. Experienced forensic accountants also can charge more per hour for their services, which is of special benefit if the professional is self-employed. With experience, a forensic accountant also may gain opportunities to manage a litigation support department or to become a partner in an accounting firm. A significant number of forensic accountants also advance by leaving larger firms to establish their own companies.

EARNINGS

While there are no annual salary statistics specifically for forensic accountants, most forensic accountants work within accounting firms and earn salaries that are commensurate with those of other accountants. According to the U.S. Department of Labor, the median annual earnings for accountants and auditors as a whole were $54,630 in 2006. The top 10 percent of accountants earned more than $94,050, and the bottom 10 percent earned less than $34,470.

According to a survey conducted by the National Association of Colleges and Employers, entry-level accountants who had bachelor's degrees received average starting salaries of $46,718 in 2006. Those with master's degrees had starting salaries of $49,277 in 2006.

General accountants and internal auditors with up to one year of experience earned between $31,500 and $48,250, according to a 2007 survey by Robert Half International. Some experienced auditors may earn between $60,000 and $208,000, depending on such factors as their education level, the size of the firm, and the firm's location. Partners in accounting firms can make even more. Naturally, salaries are affected by such factors as size of the firm, the level of the accountant's education, and any certification the accountant may have.

Government positions typically offer somewhat lower salaries than other positions. According to the U.S. Department of Labor, the average starting annual salary for junior accountants and auditors in the federal government was $28,862 in 2007. Candidates who had master's degrees or two years of experience could earn $43,731 to start. More experienced accountants in the federal government made about $78,665 per year in 2007.

As forensic accountants become more experienced, they may earn slightly more than traditional accountants because many firms tend to charge premium rates for litigation support services. A forensic accountant's salary and bonus figures usually reflect, at least to some degree, the revenue they generate for the accounting firm. For this reason, a forensic accountant's salary tends to grow as he or she gains experience. According to the National Association of Forensic Accountants, forensic accountants who had fewer than 10 years of experience charged between $80 and $140 per hour for their services. About 25 percent of those who had 11 to 15 years of experience charged between $141 and $170 per hour, and another 25 percent charged more than $170. Practitioners with between 16 and 20 years of experience charged between $171 and $200 per hour. In addition, 30 percent of those with more than 20 years of experience charged more than $200 per hour.

Most forensic accountants are employees who receive standard benefits such as paid vacation and sick days, health insurance, and 401(k) savings plans. Many who work for major accounting firms can also expect to earn bonuses based on their performance and the overall performance of their firm. Forensic accountants who become partners also may earn shares in the firm. Forensic accountants who act as self-employed consultants typically will not receive benefits and will have to provide their own health insurance and retirement plan.

WORK ENVIRONMENT

Forensic accountants typically work in bright, clean offices. A great deal of their work is done on computers and telephones, though most also occasionally travel to the offices of clients or those under investigation.

Because forensic accountants are hired to help clients prepare for trial, they often must work under tremendous pressure. They frequently encounter tight deadlines and changing schedules. Though forensic accountants generally work normal 40-hour weeks, they often work much longer hours as they prepare for a trial.

Forensic accountants also must contend with the pressures of serving as expert witnesses. Whenever they take the stand, they know that the attorneys for the other side of a case will attempt to discredit them and question their procedures and conclusions. Forensic accountants must be prepared to undergo extremely aggressive questioning. They must be able to remain calm and confident under trying circumstances.

OUTLOOK

The U.S. Department of Labor predicts the field of accounting will grow faster than the average for all occupations through 2016. As the economy grows, more accountants will be needed to prepare books and taxes for new and growing companies. New accountants also will be needed to replace those who retire or change professions. Since 1.3 million people currently work as accountants, the number of positions created by normal turnover should be significant.

The AICPA and the U.S. Department of Labor call forensic accounting one of the hot growth areas for CPAs. One reason for this may be that the job is becoming well known due to high profile cases of financial mismanagement by formerly respected accounting firms such as Arthur Andersen. In this case, forensic accountants were among the experts that investigated the financial collapse of the previously stable company Enron and determined that Arthur Andersen employees obstructed justice.

In our increasingly complex economy of business mergers, acquisitions, and failures, forensic accountants are increasingly in demand as companies rely on their services to determine if bankruptcy should be declared or if there is a way to remain solvent. The NAFA notes that the need for investigative accountants continues to increase in proportion to the insurance industry's growth and complexity. This is because insurance companies use these accountants' skills when determining how to settle claims, such as for business interruptions, inventory damage or loss, or any type of insurance claim where fraud may occur. Due to this demand, the overall outlook for forensic accountants should be good.

FOR MORE INFORMATION

Because forensic accountants are almost always certified public accountants, the AICPA is an excellent source of additional information.
American Institute of Certified Public Accountants (AICPA)
1211 Avenue of the Americas
New York, NY 10036-8775
Tel: 212-596-6200
http://www.aicpa.org

For information on scholarships, self-study courses, membership, and the CFE designation, contact
Association of Certified Fraud Examiners
The Gregor Building
716 West Avenue
Austin, TX 78701-2727
Tel: 800-245-3321
http://www.cfenet.com

For information on investigative accounting, contact
National Association of Forensic Accountants
6451 North Federal Highway, Suite 121
Fort Lauderdale, FL 33308-1487
Tel: 800-523-3680
Email: mail@nafanet.com
http://www.nafanet.com

For information on membership, scholarships, and continuing education, contact
National Society of Accountants
1010 North Fairfax Street
Alexandria, VA 22314-1504
Tel: 800-966-6679
http://www.nsacct.org

Forensic Experts

OVERVIEW

Forensic experts apply scientific principles and methods to the analysis, identification, and classification of physical evidence relating to criminal (or suspected criminal) cases. They do much of their work in laboratories, where they subject evidence to tests and then record the results. They may travel to crime scenes to collect evidence and record the physical facts of a site. Forensic experts may also be called upon to testify as expert witnesses and to present scientific findings in court.

HISTORY

In Scotland during the late 1780s, a man was convicted of murder when the soles of his boots matched a plaster cast of footprints taken from the scene of the crime. This is one of the earliest recorded cases of the use of physical evidence to link a suspected criminal with the crime.

In the late 19th century, scientists learned to analyze and classify poisons so their presence could be traced in a body. At about the same time, a controversy arose over the different methods being used to identify individuals positively. Fingerprinting emerged in the early 20th century as the most reliable method of personal identification. With the advent of X-ray technology, experts could rely on dental records to substitute for fingerprint analysis when a corpse was in advanced stages of decomposition and the condition of the skin had deteriorated.

Forensic pathology (medical examination of suspicious or unexplained deaths) also came into prominence at this time, as did ballistics, which is the study of projectiles and how they are shot from firearms. The study of ballistics was aided by the invention of the comparison microscope, which enabled an investigator to look at bullets side by side and compare their individual markings. Since individual gun barrels "scar" bullets in a unique pattern, similar markings found on different bullets may prove that they were fired from the same weapon.

These investigations by pioneer forensic scientists led the courts and the police to acknowledge the value of scientifically examined physical evidence in establishing guilt or innocence, confirming identity, proving authenticity of documents, and establishing cause of death. As the result of this acceptance by the legal and law enforcement communities, crime laboratories were established. One of the first, largest, and most complete laboratories is that of the Federal Bureau of Investigation (FBI), founded in 1932. Today, the FBI Laboratory examines many thousands of pieces of evidence each year, and its employees present their findings in trials in the United States and around the world. As the forensic sciences proved their worth, crime laboratories were established in larger cities and by state police departments. These laboratories are used in turn by many communities too small to support labs of their own. The scientific analysis of evidence has become an accepted part of police procedure, and new forensic advances, such as DNA testing, are being developed every day.

THE JOB

Forensic experts, also called *criminalists,* use the instruments of science and engineering to examine physical evidence. They use spectroscopes, microscopes, gas chromatographs, infrared and ultraviolet light, microphotography, and other lab measuring and testing equipment to analyze fibers, fabric, dust, soils, paint chips, glass fragments, fire accelerants, paper and ink, and other substances in order to identify their composition and origin. They analyze poisons, drugs, and other substances found in bodies by examining tissue samples, stomach contents, and blood samples. They analyze and classify blood, blood alcohol, semen, hair, fingernails, teeth, human and animal bones and tissue, and other biological specimens. Using samples of the DNA in these materials, they can match a person with a sample of body tissue. They study documents to determine whether they are forged or genuine. They also examine the physical properties of firearms, bullets, and explosives.

At the scene of a crime (whether actual or suspected), forensic experts collect and label evidence. This painstaking task may involve searching for spent bullets or bits of an exploded bomb and other objects scattered by an explosion. They might look for footprints, fingerprints, and tire tracks, which must be recorded or preserved by plaster casting before they are wiped out. Since crime scenes must eventually be cleaned up, forensic experts take notes and photographs to preserve the arrangement of objects, bodies, and debris. They are sometimes called on later to reconstruct the scene of a crime by making a floor plan or map pinpointing the exact location of bodies, weapons, and furniture.

One important discipline within forensic science is identification. *Fingerprint classifiers* catalog and compare fingerprints of suspected criminals with records to determine if the people who left the fingerprints at the scene of a crime were involved in previous crimes. They often try to match the fingerprints of unknown corpses with fingerprint records to establish their identities. They work in laboratories and offices, and travel to other areas such as crime scenes. Retrieving fingerprints outside may be difficult and require specialized processes, such as dusting glassware, windows, or walls with a fine powder. This powder contrasts with many different surfaces and will highlight any fingerprints that remain. Another method of retrieving fingerprints is to lift them off with a flexible tape, which can be brought back to the laboratory for further evaluation and matching.

Fingerprint classifiers compare new prints against those found after the commission of similar crimes. The classifier documents this information and transfers it to the main record-keeping system, often a large mainframe computer system. In the last decade or so, computers have greatly enhanced the possibility of matching new fingerprints to those already on file. A fingerprint classifier may keep individual files on current crimes and note any similarities between them.

Identification technicians work at various jobs related to maintaining police records. In addition to handling fingerprint records, they also work with other kinds of records, such as police reports and eyewitness information about crimes and accidents. They operate equipment used to microfilm police records, as well as store the microfilm and retrieve or copy records upon the request of police or other public officials. *Forensic pathologists* perform autopsies to determine the cause of death; autopsies are almost always performed on victims of crime. *Forensic psychiatrists* also conduct psychiatric evaluations of accused criminals and are often called to testify on whether the accused is mentally fit to stand trial.

Molecular biologists and *geneticists* analyze and review forensic and paternity samples, provide expert testimony in civil and criminal trials, and identify and develop new technologies for use in human identification.

Other job titles within forensic science include *forensic toxicologists,* who are concerned with detecting and identifying the presence of poisons or drugs in a victim's body; *forensic odontologists,* who use dental records and evidence to identify crime victims and to investigate bite marks; and *forensic anthropologists,* who examine and identify bones and skeletal remains.

Forensic experts spend the bulk of their time in the laboratory working with physical evidence. They seldom have direct contact with persons involved in actual or suspected crimes or with police investigators except when collecting evidence and reporting findings. Forensic experts do not interpret their findings relative to the criminal investigation in which they are involved; that is the work of police investigators. The purpose of crime lab work is to provide reliable scientific analysis of evidence that can then be used in criminal investigations and, if needed later, in court proceedings.

REQUIREMENTS

High School
Almost all jobs in this field require at least a bachelor's degree. In high school, you can begin to prepare for a career in forensics by taking a heavy concentration of science courses, including chemistry, biology, physiology, and physics. Computer skills are also important, especially for fingerprint classifiers. A basic grounding in spoken and written communications will be useful because forensic experts must write very detailed reports and are sometimes called on to present their findings in court.

Postsecondary Training
A number of universities and community colleges in the United States offer programs in forensic science, odontology, toxicology, forensic accounting, pathology, and various aspects of crime lab work. These courses are often spread throughout the school, in the anatomy, physiology, chemistry, or biology departments, or they may be grouped together as part of the criminal justice department. Additionally, some colleges may have separate forensic science departments. Visit the Web sites of the American Academy of Forensic Sciences (http://www.aafs.org) and the Council on Forensic Science Education (http://www.criminology.fsu.edu/COFSE/default. html) for lists of colleges and universities that offer classes and programs in forensic science.

Certification or Licensing
Certification may be an advantage for people working in toxicology and document examination. Specialists in these and other disciplines may also be required to take undergraduate and graduate course

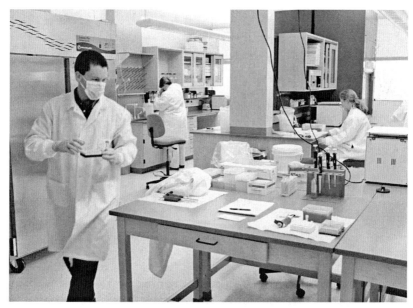

Forensic experts at the FBI Laboratory perform the early stages of mitochondrial DNA extraction. *(Charles Dharapak, AP Images)*

work in their areas. In a field such as toxicology, advanced chemistry work is important.

Other Requirements

To be successful in this field, you should have an aptitude for scientific investigation, an inquiring and logical mind, and the ability to make precise measurements and observations. Patience and persistence are important qualities, as is a good memory. Forensic experts must constantly bear in mind that the accuracy of their lab investigations can have great consequences for others.

EXPLORING

A large community police department may have a crime lab of its own whose experts can give you specific information about their work and the preparation that helped them build their careers. Smaller communities often use the lab facilities of a larger city nearby or the state police. A school counselor or a representative of the local police may be able to help you arrange a tour of these labs. Lectures in forensic science given at universities or police conventions may also be open to students. Online services and Internet access may provide entry to forums devoted to forensic science and are good sources of information on the daily and professional experiences of people already active in this field.

EMPLOYERS

Forensic scientists are typically employed by large police departments or state law enforcement agencies nationwide. However, individuals in certain disciplines are often self-employed or work in the private sector. For example, *forensic engineers,* who use mathematical principles to reconstruct accident scenes, determine the origins of explosions and fires, or review the design of chemical or molecular structures, may be employed by large corporations, small firms, or government agencies. Forensic anthropologists, who identify skeletal remains, may work within a university or college, teaching related courses, conducting research, and consulting on cases submitted by law enforcement agencies. They may also be employed by the federal government (including the FBI and the military) or a medical examiner's office. Many forensic science concentrations also offer part-time or consulting opportunities, depending on your level of education and experience.

STARTING OUT

Crime labs are maintained by the federal government and by state and local governments. Applications should be made directly to the personnel department of the government agency supporting the lab. Civil service appointments usually require applicants to take an examination. Such appointments are usually widely advertised well in advance of the application date. Those working for the FBI or other law enforcement agencies usually undergo background checks, which examine their character, background, previous employers, and family and friends.

ADVANCEMENT

In a large crime laboratory, forensic technicians usually advance from an assistant's position to working independently at one or more special types of analysis. From there they may advance to a position as project leader or being in charge of all aspects of one particular investigation. In smaller labs, one technician may have to fill many roles. With experience, such a technician may progress to more responsible work but receive no advancement in title. Fingerprint classifiers who work for police departments may pursue advancement with a different government agency or apply for positions with the FBI.

Crucial to advancement is further education. Forensic experts need to be familiar with scientific procedures such as gas chromatography, ultraviolet and infrared spectrophotometry, mass spectroscopy, electrophoresis, polarizing microscopy, light microscopy, and conventional and isoelectric focusing; knowledge of these analytical techniques and procedures is taught or more fully explored at the master's and doctorate levels. Other, more specific areas of forensics, such as DNA analysis, require advanced degrees in molecular biology and genetics.

EARNINGS

Earnings for forensic experts vary with the employer, geographic location, and educational and skill levels. Salaries for entry-level positions as research assistants or technicians working in local and regional labs range from $20,000 to $25,000. For those individuals with a bachelor's degree and two to five years of specialized experience, salaries range from $30,000 to $40,000. Salaries for those with advanced degrees range from $50,000 to well over $100,000 a year. The U.S. Department of Labor reports that the median hourly salary for forensic science technicians was $21.79 in 2006. For full-time employment, this means a median salary of approximately $45,330 a year.

Benefits for full-time workers include vacation and sick time, health, and (sometimes) dental insurance, and pension or 401 (k) plans.

WORK ENVIRONMENT

Forensic experts usually perform the analytical portion of their work in clean, quiet, air-conditioned laboratories, but they are frequently required to travel to crime scenes to collect evidence or study the site to understand more fully the evidence collected by detectives. When gathering evidence and analyzing it, forensic experts need to be able to concentrate, sometimes in crowded, noisy situations. For this reason, forensic experts must be adaptable and able to work in a variety of environments, including dangerous or unpleasant places.

Many crime scenes are grisly and may be extremely distressing for beginning workers and even for more seasoned professionals. In addition, forensic experts who work with human remains will regularly view corpses, and, more often than not, these corpses will have been mutilated in some way or be in varying degrees of decomposition. Individuals interested in this field need to develop the detachment and objectivity necessary to view corpses and extract specimens for testing and analysis.

Simulating the precise conditions of a crime site for a full analysis is often crucial, so forensic experts often return to the site so that they can perform tests or functions outside of the controlled environment of their lab. When traveling to the scene of a crime, forensic experts may have to carry cases of tools, cameras, and chemicals. In order not to risk contaminating evidence, they must follow strict procedures (both in and out of the laboratory) for collecting and testing evidence; these procedures can be extremely time-consuming and thus require a great deal of patience. Forensic experts also need to be able to arrive at and present their findings impartially. In large labs, they often work as part of a team under the direction of a senior technologist. They may experience eyestrain and contact with strong chemicals, but little heavy physical work is involved.

OUTLOOK

The employment of forensic experts is expected to grow much faster than the average for all occupations through 2016, according to the U.S. Department of Labor. Population increases, a rising crime rate, and the greater emphasis on scientific methodology in crime investigation have increased the need for trained experts. Forensic experts who are employed by state and local public safety departments should experience especially strong employment opportunities, although some government agencies may be under pressure to reduce staff because of budget problems. Forensic experts with a four-year degree in forensic science will enjoy the best employment prospects.

FOR MORE INFORMATION

For information on careers and colleges and universities that offer forensic science programs, contact
American Academy of Forensic Sciences
410 North 21st Street
Colorado Springs, CO 80904-2798
Tel: 719-636-1100
http://www.aafs.org

To learn more about forensic services at the FBI, visit the FBI Laboratory Division's Web site.
Federal Bureau of Investigation (FBI)
J. Edgar Hoover Building
935 Pennsylvania Avenue
Washington, DC 20535-0001

Tel: 202-324-3000
http://www.fbi.gov and http://www.fbi.gov/hq/lab/labhome.htm

For additional information on forensics and forensics professionals, contact the following organizations
American Society of Questioned Document Examiners
PO Box 18298
Long Beach, CA 90807-8298
http://www.asqde.org

Society of Forensic Toxicologists
One MacDonald Center
1 North MacDonald Street, Suite 15
Mesa, AZ 85201-7340
Tel: 888-866-7638
Email: office@soft-tox.org
http://www.soft-tox.org

For information on colleges and universities that offer forensic science programs, contact
Council on Forensic Science Education
http://www.criminology.fsu.edu/COFSE/default.html

INTERVIEW

Timothy Palmbach is an associate professor and the chair of the Forensic Science Department at the University of New Haven (http://www.newhaven.edu/5765) in West Haven, Connecticut. He discussed his career and the education of forensic science students with the editors of Careers in Focus: Law.

Q. Can you tell us about your program and your background?

A. At the University of New Haven we offer both undergraduate and graduate degree programs in forensic science. The B.S. Forensic Science degree is an academically rigorous program devoted heavily to the natural sciences. By their junior year students elect either a forensic biology or forensic chemistry track. In fact, many students are able to earn dual bachelor degrees—often a B.S. Chemistry or B.S. Biology degree—in addition to their forensic science degree. Graduate students earn an M.S. Forensic Science with one of two concentrations: criminalistics or advanced investigation.

Criminalistics students are being trained to be forensic science laboratory personnel and usually have undergraduate degrees in biology or chemistry. Advanced investigation students learn about forensic science disciplines, but focus more on how to apply these principles for investigative or crime scene analysis purposes.

My early ambitions were to be a police officer. In the late 1970s I somehow stumbled onto this relatively unknown field of forensic science. Learning science in an applied manner, that is to solve crime, quickly captured my passion. I completed my undergraduate studies at the University of New Haven with a B.S. Forensic Science degree as well as a B.S. Chemistry degree. I did not realize at the time that I would have the gift of being mentored for my entire career by the new program director, Dr. Henry Lee [an internationally renowned forensic scientist].

After graduation I took a job with the Connecticut State Police and spent a great deal of time doing crime scene analysis and investigations. Educationally, I next obtained a M.S. Forensic Science degree from the University of New Haven. Finally, I went to the University of Connecticut School of Law and earned a juris doctor degree. The last portion of my career with Connecticut was in the Forensic Science Laboratory. In 2004 I retired as the director and commanding officer for the Division of Scientific Services in Connecticut. My career then went full circle and I returned to where it had all begun for me some 25 years earlier. Currently, I am an associate professor and chair of the Forensic Science Department. It is a great joy and honor to help wonderful, bright, and dedicated students find their own path into a field that has been both fulfilling and challenging throughout.

Q. What is one thing that young people may not know about a career in forensic science?

A. CSI and the general pop culture fascination with forensic science and crime scene analysis have been both a blessing and a source of several problems within the related subdisciplines. For those of us in the field, we have gone from a career of obscurity to a focal point at a cocktail party. People are generally informed and interested in both fact and fiction as they relate to true crime as well as fiction. As a result, colleges have enjoyed a supply of exceptional science-oriented students in forensic science majors. Gifted students who otherwise may have elected other areas of study have realized that an applied science such as forensic science is downright fun! However, one potential problem with this public interest is that jurors often enter a trial with misperceptions or unrealistic expectations that must be addressed by the scientist who will appear before them. Only on prime time television can a complex murder be fully resolved within the commercial breaks and every piece of evidence providing the precise answer necessary to solve the caper.

For young people aspiring to a career in forensic science, the most common misperception is a lack of understanding that forensic science is first and foremost science. Only after a student has mastered many of the basic principles in chemistry, biology, physics, and mathematics will they be prepared to learn the analytical methods necessary to examine evidence associated with a criminal or civil case. Thus, with quality programs they find themselves challenged by rigorous curriculum for two years, before they have an opportunity to begin applying this knowledge in a forensic science discipline. Perhaps the other great unknown is that most individuals outside of the field have a limited view of the diversity and scope of the many sub-disciplines in forensic science. Virtually any of the existing scientific fields have direct application to forensic science. Therefore, a student could aspire to a more traditional role such as DNA analyst, but they could also find a niche in an area such as forensic engineering.

Q. What types of students pursue study in your program?

A. There are some common personality traits that are good indicators of success within this field. Do you like to look for small pieces to solve a big puzzle? Are you well organized, methodical, and do you pay attention to small details? Are you a patient person? Ideally, you answered yes to each of these questions. Further, in high school have you enjoyed and excelled in chemistry, biology, physics, and math (including trigonometry and pre-calculus/calculus)? Finally, be aware that forensic science is all about science. It must be done in an objective and unbiased manner. Anyone choosing a career in this field must always demonstrate integrity and ethical behavior. However, this is one of the most rewarding and forever progressing fields that you could choose. This is not a choice you will regret.

Q. What advice would you offer forensic science majors as they graduate and look for jobs?

A. Good students who are dedicated, persistent, and flexible can realize a successful career path. Over the last few years the job market has become quite competitive, so students need to set themselves apart from the competition. As you evaluate the many academic options, seek a quality, time-proven, and reputable program. Criteria such as program accreditation, length of time the program has been in place, and number of successful graduates are some key elements worthy of consideration. In addition, students should seek programs where the majority of faculty have solid academic credentials, but also have practical experience working within the field. Since forensic science is an applied science it is imperative that students be taught by professors who actually faced the daily challenges faced by a modern bench-level forensic scientist. During his or her education a student should also seek opportunities to engage in an internship program within a real forensic science laboratory. Participation in scientific research is another excellent way to further a student's learning and resume. Finally, most students need to realize that this field, like many others, requires one to enter the field where one can and work toward your ultimate career goal.

Q. Are there any changes in this job market that students should expect? Have certain areas of this field been especially promising (or on the decline) in recent years?

A. Many students will obtain their first job in a private or research laboratory where they can gain additional experience and training that will make them a better candidate for the crime lab job of their dreams. Historically, drug analysis and DNA testing are the disciplines that hire the most at entry levels. Many forensic scientists began their career in one of these major disciplines and then over time transitioned into another area of the forensic laboratory, such as trace evidence. However, in general the field of forensic science has become more specialized and there are fewer opportunities for a generalist type of career track. Digital forensics, or the examination of a multitude of forms of electronic or computer evidence, is an area that has realized a great deal of recent growth. This area is also advantageous in that many jobs can be found within the private sector, thus expanding the job market. Some of the identification or physical methods disciplines, such as firearms examiners, have come in short supply. However, these areas require a great deal of apprenticeship and training before a forensic laboratory can utilize these individuals in case work. In general, a student who is well prepared with a strong science background, chemistry or biology, will have the basic skills required to obtain and succeed in a traditional forensic science position.

Q. **What is one of your most rewarding experiences in the field, and why?**

A. Simply, I am utterly amazed as to the extent of which a career in forensic science has challenged me, rewarded me, entertained me, changed me, and hopefully allowed me an opportunity to serve others. Forensic scientists are advocates for justice. Forensic scientists have the privilege of using the best science has to offer to help solve a crime, make society safer, exonerate the innocent, and provide guidance for issues involving social justice and political unrest. Over my career I have been exposed to the inhumanity of crime, horrors of war such as mass graves in Bosnia, assassination attempts of national leaders, and cases of pure historical significance. If you commit to the rigors of forensic science, you will go places and see things you never imagined—and certainly never get bored!

Intellectual Property Lawyers

QUICK FACTS

School Subjects
English
Government
Speech

Personal Skills
Communication/ideas
Leadership/management

Work Environment
Primarily indoors
Primarily multiple locations

Minimum Education Level
Law degree

Salary Range
$77,000 to $119,000 to
$200,000+

Certification or Licensing
Required

Outlook
Faster than the average

DOT
110

GOE
04.02.01

NOC
4112

O*NET-SOC
23-1011.00

OVERVIEW

Intellectual property (IP) lawyers focus on the protection of creative thought. IP lawyers may work with patents to protect their clients' inventions and discoveries; copyrights to protect works their clients have authored, such as music or computer programs; and trademarks to protect brand names and symbols associated with their clients' businesses. IP attorneys may also work with companies to protect their trade secrets. IP lawyers are kept busy during periods of economic productivity, protecting emerging new ideas and creations such as Internet sites and scientific discoveries. According to the Franklin Pierce Law Center, the United States is the largest producer of intellectual property in the world.

HISTORY

Ever since the 1300s, people have sought help to protect their ideas. Unfortunately, in the past both lawyers and clients were often frustrated in their attempts to gain support for patents and copyrights in court. The country as a whole, the court system, and Congress were intent on not allowing monopolies to gain control of innovative products or ideas. This fear of monopolization caused the patent holder to get little if any help or protection from the government. Within the past 25 years, however, Congress and judges have started to see innovative ideas and products as valuable for U.S. trade status in the international market.

Attitudes are not the only things that have changed. Compared to the earliest years of inventions, innovative ideas, and patent seeking, huge amounts of intellectual property are now created and need protection daily. Intellectual property now includes music, computer software, written documents, programming code, and much more. Just as the volume and type of intellectual property has grown, so have the ways to steal it. Thieves today use home computers, digital equipment, and satellites. This boom in intellectual property and its need for protection have increased the demand for IP lawyers. Previously, IP law was a smaller segment of a law firm's business, so it was hired out to smaller boutique-type law firms. Now major firms and corporations have entire teams in-house to meet the demands of intellectual law.

The Internet has also been instrumental in creating a demand for these lawyers as they try to protect the use of online material.

THE JOB

Intellectual property lawyers protect a client's creative interests, whether those interests are to patent a new product or to ensure that a copyright hasn't been infringed upon. IP lawyers may work in all areas of intellectual property law; however, many lawyers specialize in patent, trademark, copyright, or licensing law. (For more on careers in patent law, see Patent Lawyers.) Whichever area the IP attorney focuses on, some job duties are the same across the board. One of the IP lawyer's main tasks is to counsel clients. Usually this counseling concerns whether the intellectual property can be patented, trademarked, or copyrighted; the best method of protection for the individual property; and whether the product or idea being discussed will infringe on someone else's patent, trademark, or copyright. Another major task for an IP lawyer is the drafting of legal documents, such as patent applications and licensing agreements. Registered patent attorney Delbert Phillips states, "An IP lawyer drafts applications to the Patent Office and answers actions from the United States Patent Office by way of drafting amendments to the already filed application. Also, part of the job is drafting licenses and assignments (papers transferring ownership or giving permission for other people to practice the invention) for patent and trademarks."

The IP lawyer also serves clients by being their advocate before administrative bodies and courts. The IP lawyer's goal is to secure the rights of the client and then protect those rights if others violate them. Conversely, if the IP lawyer's client is accused of violating someone else's intellectual property rights, the IP lawyer defends the client.

IP lawyers may help their clients choose an Internet domain name or a trademark. They are often called upon to review advertising copy, press releases, and other official documents to ensure that there are no intellectual property problems.

IP lawyers work with a wide variety of clients, from an individual inventor or author to the highest manager of a large corporation. Those who work for corporations are usually in-house counsels concerned with decisions affecting the use of intellectual property within the company. IP lawyers working in universities assist scientists and researchers by identifying products and inventions that have potential in the marketplace.

The majority of IP lawyers focus on patent law. A patent lawyer works with an inventor from the beginning to decide if the invention has a chance of being granted a patent. If so, the attorney drafts and files a patent application with the United States Patent Office. The lawyer then works with the patent examiner to try to get the patent approved. If a patent is issued, the lawyer has succeeded; if it is not, the attorney can appeal the decision to the Patent Office's board of appeals. If the lawyer and client are again denied a patent, they can appeal to the United States Court of Appeals for the Federal Circuit. Once a patent is approved, the patent lawyer may continue to be involved by investigating and developing licensing agreements.

If a client believes his or her rights to intellectual property have been infringed upon, the IP attorney must try to prove that someone else has taken or used the client's intellectual property without consent. On the other hand, if a client is accused of infringing on another's intellectual property rights, the lawyer must try to prove that the item in question didn't deserve a copyright, patent, or trademark in the first place or that the protection is invalid. Although lawsuits are commonplace today, most IP lawyers consider litigation the last step and try to settle differences outside the courtroom.

REQUIREMENTS
High School
Because intellectual property often deals with creations in the scientific, engineering, literary, and music worlds, a background in any of those areas will be helpful. If you are interested in combining a certain area with practicing law, you should focus on that area while in high school. "Take as many science courses as possible along with technical writing," recommends Delbert Phillips. "An IP lawyer must know basic scientific principles in order to draft the patent applications. It also helps if the student can become meticulous in thinking and in keeping track of records." Take courses in business, accounting, English, computers, and government as well.

Postsecondary Training

As in other areas of law, IP lawyers most often complete an undergraduate degree and then graduate from law school. For most types of intellectual property law, the undergraduate degree does not have to be in a specific major. The exception to that is patent law. If you want to become a patent lawyer, you should major in science, engineering, or physics. Other technology-related courses will also be helpful.

To apply for almost any law school, you must first pass the Law School Admission Test (LSAT). The LSAT is an aptitude test used to predict how successful an individual will be in law school. Most law schools teach courses in intellectual property law, but some have IP sections and degrees, such as Columbia Law School, Franklin Pierce Law Center, and George Mason University School of Law.

Certification or Licensing

After graduating from law school, you will be eligible to take the bar exam in any state. After passing the bar, you will be sworn in as an attorney and will then be eligible to practice law. Patent attorneys who practice patent law before the United States Patent Office must go a step further and obtain additional certification. Would-be patent lawyers must pass the patent bar exam. According to the American Bar Association, you must hold a bachelor's degree in engineering, physics, or the natural sciences (such as chemistry and biochemistry), hold a bachelor's degree in another subject, or have passed the Engineer in Training test in order to be eligible to take the patent bar exam.

Other Requirements

IP lawyers should have excellent written and oral communication skills. In fact, the American Bar Foundation says a recent survey shows that law firms are more interested in these skills than the overall legal knowledge of the interviewee. Also, having command of foreign languages is crucial because IP lawyers work with products and ideas in international markets.

Phillips says that a patent lawyer who practices solo must be "a generalist who can understand mechanical engineering, basic electrical engineering, and rudimentary chemistry in order to draft the application and argue the merits during the amendment phase of intellectual law."

EXPLORING

IP law is a perfect career for someone who is interested in both science and technology and legal areas. Because of this duality, you can explore the career by focusing on the law side or on the science/ technology side. To get experience on the law side, seek summer jobs and internships with law offices where you live. You may be able to get a part-time job as a legal assistant. Also check out your local business college for special pre-law programs that offer introductory law courses to the public. If you can't get any hands-on experience right away, ask your guidance counselor for help in setting up a tour of a local law office or arranging for an interview with a law professional. Any experience you can get writing technical or legal documents can also help, so don't rule out temporary jobs in any kind of business office.

If you have another interest that you hope to combine with law, try to get some hands-on experience in that area as well. If you are interested in science, for instance, join the science club at your school. Ask your science teacher about planning a field trip to anywhere you can learn about engineering. Take initiative and start an inventors club with your classmates to come up with new ideas and products.

EMPLOYERS

Intellectual property lawyers are in high demand with many types of employers. You'll find IP lawyers in major corporations, law firms, universities, and government agencies. IP lawyers may also own their own businesses. The main employer of IP attorneys, however, is the United States Patent and Trademark Office (USPTO), which is part of the Department of Commerce. The USPTO employs lawyers as trademark examiners, patent examiners, and more. Other departments in the government that employ IP lawyers include the Departments of Defense, Interior, Justice, and Energy. IP lawyers can also find employment in the United States Copyright Office.

Although IP lawyers are in high demand all over the country, most work in large cities where the major corporations are headquartered. Other hot spots for IP lawyers include Washington, D.C., because of the government agencies located there, and Silicon Valley, California, because of its concentration of computer-related industry.

STARTING OUT

As in any area of law, internships and clerkships are usually the path to a quality job. For those interested in patent law specifically, applying for a clerkship in the United States Court of Appeals for the Federal Court in Washington, D.C., is a great way to gain experience. To apply for an unpaid, part-time internship during law school or soon after graduation, you should write directly to the court about six months in advance. To gain a full-time, paid clerkship position, law students should inquire sometime before the end of their second year. You can also apply for clerkships and internships with law firms. Another way to break into the IP law field is to get a job at the USPTO. Working directly with patents will put you in a better position for an IP job later in your career.

ADVANCEMENT

Most IP lawyers start out with internships and clerkships at firms or courts. In law firms, IP lawyers start out as low-rung associates and then advance as their experience and track records allow. Associates with successful reputations and many years of experience can become partners in the law firm. IP lawyers who work for universities may advance from assisting scientific and engineering groups to becoming professors of IP law. Whether in corporations, government agencies, or law firms, most IP lawyers, like other types of lawyers, are given more high profile cases and more important clients as they become more experienced.

EARNINGS

According to the American Intellectual Property Law Association, the average salary for an IP attorney in corporate offices and patent firms is $119,000 per year. Inexperienced IP lawyers can expect to make between $80,000 and $85,000, and those with the most experience and success will earn more than $180,000 per year. The median income for partners in private law firms is over $200,000 per year, while associates' salary is about $77,000. IP lawyers who own their own practices usually make $100,000 per year while salaries for those who work in law firms and corporations averaged slightly higher.

Almost all corporations, firms, and government agencies provide medical insurance, vacation, sick days, and holidays. Partners in large firms can expect other perks as well, including company cars, spending allowances, bonuses, and more depending on the firm.

WORK ENVIRONMENT

IP attorneys, like lawyers in other areas, have heavy workloads and work long hours. IP lawyers may spend hours poring over documents with few breaks. Many law firms have weekly goals for their lawyers that include the number of hours billed to the client. Some of these goals can be extremely demanding. Most of the lawyer's time is spent indoors meeting with clients, researching, or arguing in court. Depending on their position in the company or firm, IP lawyers may lead a team of lawyers or supervise a group of paralegals and associates.

OUTLOOK

The outlook for intellectual property law is promising. This field is relatively new and the demand for IP professionals doesn't show signs of slowing. The growth of the computer industry and the Internet has provided a great amount of work for IP lawyers. As new computer software and online media enters the market, IP lawyers will be needed to protect it. According to the American Bar Association, even if other markets that use the services of lawyers are softened by recession, the demand for IP lawyers will remain high. Because there will always be a need to protect the creative resources of the people, there will also be a need for IP lawyers.

FOR MORE INFORMATION

For information on all areas of law, law schools, the bar exam, and career guidance, contact
American Bar Association
321 North Clark Street
Chicago, IL 60610-4714
Tel: 800-285-2221
Email: askaba@abanet.org
http://www.abanet.org

To read the publications What Is a Patent, a Trademark and a Copyright? *and* Careers in IP Law, *visit the AIPLA's Web site.*
American Intellectual Property Law Association (AIPLA)
241 18th Street South, Suite 700
Arlington, VA 22202-3419
Tel: 703-415-0780
Email: aipla@aipla.org
http://www.aipla.org

For information about IP law and degree programs, contact
Franklin Pierce Law Center
2 White Street
Concord, NH 03301-4176

Tel: 603-228-1541
Email: admissions@piercelaw.edu
http://www.fplc.edu

For information on patent law, contact
National Association of Patent Practitioners
4680-18-i Monticello Avenue
PMB 101
Williamsburg, VA 23188-8214
Tel: 800-216-9588
Email: napp@napp.org
http://www.napp.org

For information about IP, job opportunities, and recent press releases, contact the USPTO. Its Web site offers a link designed specifically for creative students interested in invention and includes contest information.
United States Patent and Trademark Office (USPTO)
Office of Public Affairs
PO Box 1450
Alexandria, VA 22313-1450
Tel: 800-786-9199
Email: usptoinfo@uspto.gov
http://www.uspto.gov

Judges

QUICK FACTS

School Subjects
English
Government
Speech

Personal Skills
Communication/ideas
Leadership/management

Work Environment
Primarily indoors
Primarily multiple locations

Minimum Education Level
Bachelor's degree

Salary Range
$29,540 to $101,690 to
$217,400

Certification or Licensing
Required

Outlook
More slowly than the average

DOT
111

GOE
04.02.01

NOC
4111

O*NET-SOC
23-1021.00, 23-1023.00

OVERVIEW

Judges are elected or appointed officials who preside over federal, state, county, and municipal courts. They apply the law to citizens and businesses and oversee court proceedings according to the established law. Judges also give new rulings on issues not previously decided. Approximately 51,000 judges work in all levels of the judiciary arm of the United States.

HISTORY

The tradition of governing people by laws has been established over centuries. Societies have built up systems of law that have been studied and drawn upon by later governments. The earliest known law is the Code of Hammurabi, developed about 1800 B.C. by the ruler of the Sumerians. Another early set of laws was the law of Moses, known as the Ten Commandments. Much modern European law was organized and refined by legal experts assembled by Napoleon; their body of law was known as the Napoleonic Code. English colonists coming to America brought English common law, from which American laws have grown. In areas of the United States that were heavily settled by Spanish colonists, there are traces of Spanish law.

The Constitution of the United States, which was first adopted in 1787, is the supreme law of the land. It created three branches of government—executive, legislative, and judicial—to act as checks upon one another. It also stipulated that "[t]he judicial Power of the United States, shall be vested in one supreme Court, and in such inferior Courts as the Congress from time to time ordain and establish." The Supreme Court was created by the Judiciary Act of September 24, 1789. The Supreme Court is the highest court of the land and rules on issues related to the U.S. Constitution. The Supreme Court is made up of nine justices, appointed by the president with consent of the Senate, who review selected decisions made at the state level.

The Circuit Court of Appeals deals with appeals of decisions made by the district courts and reviews judgments of lower courts.

The district courts are the third level of the federal court system, servicing approximately 100 zones, or districts, across the country.

Each state also has its own judicial system, which is separate from the federal system. Most civil and criminal cases are tried in state courts. These cases can move on to a federal court if they are related to an issue concerning the U.S. Constitution. Most cities also have municipal courts to handle minor cases.

THE JOB

Judges are most often lawyers who have either been elected or appointed to preside over federal, state, county, or municipal courts. Federal and state judges are usually required to have a law degree; approximately 40 states allow those with a bachelor's degree and work experience to hold limited-jurisdiction judgeships.

Judges administer court procedures during trials and hearings and establish new rules on questions where standard procedures have not previously been set. They read or listen to claims made by parties involved in civil suits and make decisions based on facts, applicable statutes, and prior court decisions. They examine evidence in criminal cases to see if it supports the charges. Judges listen to the presentation of cases, rule on the admission of evidence and testimony, and settle disputes between attorneys. They instruct juries on their duties and advise them of laws that apply to the case. They sentence defendants found guilty of criminal charges and decide who is responsible in nonjury civil cases. Besides their work in the courtroom, judges also research legal matters, study prior rulings, write opinions, and keep abreast of legislation that may affect their rulings.

Some judges have other titles such as *magistrate,* or *justice,* and preside over a limited jurisdiction. Magistrates hear civil cases in which damages do not exceed a prescribed maximum, as well as minor misdemeanor cases that do not involve penitentiary sentences or fines that exceed a certain specified amount.

REQUIREMENTS

High School

Most judges first work as lawyers before being elected or appointed to the bench. A high school diploma, a college degree, and three years of law school are minimum requirements for a law degree. A high school diploma is the first step in a lawyer's education. If you are considering a career in law, courses such as government, history, social studies, and economics provide a solid background for entering college-level courses. Speech courses are also helpful to build strong communication skills necessary for the profession. Also take advantage of any computer-related classes or experience you can get, because lawyers and judges often use technology to research and interpret the law, from surfing the Internet to searching legal databases.

Postsecondary Training

To enter any law school approved by the American Bar Association, you must satisfactorily complete at least three, and usually four, years of college work. Most law schools do not specify any particular courses for prelaw education. Usually a liberal arts track is most advisable, with courses in English, history, economics, social sciences, logic, and public speaking. A college student planning on specialization in a particular area of law, however, might also take courses significantly related to that area, such as economics, agriculture, or political science. Those interested should contact several law schools to learn more about any requirements and to see if they will accept credits from the college the student is planning to attend.

Currently, 195 law schools in the United States are approved by the American Bar Association; others, many of them night schools, are approved by state authorities only. Most of the approved law schools, however, do have night sessions to accommodate part-time students. Part-time courses of study usually take four years to complete.

Law school training consists of required courses such as legal writing and research, contracts, criminal law, constitutional law, torts, and property. The second and third years may be devoted to specialized courses of interest to the student, such as evidence, business transactions and corporations, or admiralty. The study of cases and decisions is of basic importance to the law student, who will be required to read and study thousands of these cases. A degree of juris doctor (JD) or bachelor of laws (LLB) is usually granted upon graduation. Some law students considering specialization, research, or teaching may go on for advanced study.

Most law schools require that applicants take the Law School Admission Test (LSAT), where prospective law students are tested on their critical thinking, writing, and reasoning abilities.

Certification or Licensing

Every state requires that lawyers be admitted to the bar of that state before they can practice. Applicants for the bar must have graduated from an approved law school and pass a written examination in the state in which they intend to practice. In a few states, graduates of law schools within the state are excused from these written examinations. After lawyers have been admitted to the bar in one state, they can practice in another state without taking a written examination if the states have reciprocity agreements; however, they will be required to meet certain state standards of good character and legal experience and pay any applicable fees.

There is no specific certification or licensing available for judges.

Other Requirements

Federal courts and agencies have their own rules regulating admission to practice. Other requirements vary among the states. For example, the states of Vermont, New York, Washington, Virginia, California, Maine, and Wyoming allow a person who has spent several years reading law in a law office but has no college training or who has a combination of reading and law school experience to take the state bar examination. However, few people now enter law practice in this manner.

A few states accept the study of law by correspondence. Some states require that newly graduated lawyers serve a period of clerkship in an established law firm before they are eligible to take the bar examination.

Almost all judges appointed or elected to any court must be lawyers and members of the bar, usually with many years of experience.

Both lawyers and judges have to be effective communicators, work well with people, and be able to find creative solutions to problems, such as complex court cases.

EXPLORING

If you think a career as a lawyer or judge might be right up your alley, there are several ways you can find out more about it before making that final decision. First, sit in on a trial or two at your local or state courthouse. Try to focus mainly on the judge and the lawyer and take note of what they do. Write down questions you have and terms or actions you don't understand. Then, talk to your guidance counselor and ask for help in setting up a telephone or in-person interview with a judge or lawyer. Ask questions and get the scoop on what those careers are really all about. Also, talk to your guidance counselor or political science teacher about starting or joining a job shadowing program. Job shadowing programs allow you to follow a person in a certain career around for a day or two to get an idea of what goes on in a typical day. You may even be invited to help out with a few minor duties.

You can also search the World Wide Web for general information about lawyers and judges and current court cases. Read court transcripts and summary opinions written by judges on issues of importance today. After you've done some research and talked to a lawyer or judge and you still think you are destined for law school, try to get a part-time job in a law office. Ask your guidance counselor for help.

If you are already in law school, you might consider becoming a student member of the American Bar Association. Student members receive *Student Lawyer,* a magazine that contains useful information for aspiring lawyers. Read sample articles from the magazine at http://www.abanet.org/lsd/studentlawyer.

EMPLOYERS

Approximately 51,000 judges are employed in the United States. Judges and magistrates work for federal, state, and local levels of government. About 53 percent of all judges work for state and local government.

STARTING OUT

The career of judge is not an entry-level position. Judges typically start out as lawyers and are appointed or elected to the bench only after years of experience and careful study of the law.

The first steps in entering the law profession are graduation from an approved law school and passing a state bar examination. Beginning lawyers usually work as assistants to experienced lawyers. At first they do mainly research and routine work. After a few years of successful experience, they may be ready to go out on their own. Other choices open to the beginning lawyer include joining an established law firm or entering into partnership with another lawyer.

ADVANCEMENT

Judges usually advance from lower courts to higher courts either in terms of the matters that are decided or in terms of the level—local, state, or federal.

EARNINGS

Judges earned median annual salaries of $101,690 in 2006, according to the U.S. Department of Labor. Salaries ranged from less than $29,540 to more than $135,010.

According to the Administrative Office of the U.S. Courts, federal district court judges earned an average of $169,300 in 2008. The chief justice of the United States earned $217,400, while associate justices of the Supreme Court earned $208,100 in 2008. A survey conducted by the National Center for State Courts reports the 2007 average salaries for associate judges in the states' highest courts ranged from $106,185 to $209,521. At the state level, judges serving in intermediate appellate courts earned salaries that ranged from $105,050 to $196,428, and in general jurisdiction trial courts, salaries ranged from $99,234 to $171,648.

Judges usually receive paid vacations and holidays, sick leave, hospitalization and insurance benefits, and pension programs.

WORK ENVIRONMENT

Courtrooms are usually pleasant, although busy, places to work. Some courts, such as small claims, family, or surrogate, may have evening hours to provide flexibility to the community. Criminal arraignments may be held at any time of the day or night. Court hours for most judges are usually regular business hours, with a one-hour lunch break.

OUTLOOK

Employment of judges is expected to grow more slowly than the average for all occupations through 2016, according to the U.S. Department of Labor. Budgetary cuts may limit the hiring of new judges at all levels—but especially at the federal level. Despite this prediction, demand for judges should grow as the public focuses more on crime, as well as seeks to litigate disputes that were previously handled out of court. Employment will also grow as a result of demographic shifts in the U.S. population; more judges will be needed to handle immigration- and elder law-related issues. Medical science, electronic commerce, information technology, and globalization are other areas in which judges will be needed. Most positions will open as judges retire or leave the field to go into the private sector (which is more lucrative). There may be an increase in judges in cities with large population growth, but competition will be high for any openings.

FOR MORE INFORMATION

For information about law student services offered by the ABA,
contact
American Bar Association (ABA)
321 North Clark Street
Chicago, IL 60610-4714
Tel: 800-285-2221
Email: askaba@abanet.org
http://www.abanet.org

For information on AALS members and workshops and seminars,
contact
Association of American Law Schools
1201 Connecticut Avenue, NW, Suite 800
Washington, DC 20036-2717
Tel: 202-296-8851
Email: aals@aals.org
http://www.aals.org

The FBA provides information for lawyers and judges involved in
federal practice.
Federal Bar Association (FBA)
Student Services
2011 Crystal Drive, Suite 400
Arlington, VA 22202-3709
Tel: 703-682-7000
Email: fba@fedbar.org
http://fedbar.org

For information on educational programs for federal judges,
contact
Federal Judicial Center
Thurgood Marshall Federal Judiciary Building
One Columbus Circle, NE
Washington DC 200022-8003
Tel: 202-502-4000
http://www.fjc.gov

For information on choosing a law school, law careers, salaries, and
alternative law careers, contact
National Association for Law Placement
1025 Connecticut Avenue, NW, Suite 1110
Washington, DC 20036-5413

Tel: 202-835-1001
Email: info@nalp.org
http://www.nalp.org

For information on state courts, contact
National Center for State Courts
2425 Wilson Boulevard, Suite 350
Arlington, VA 22201-3320
http://www.ncsconline.org

For information on judicial education, contact
National Judicial College
University of Nevada-Reno
Judicial College Building, MS 358
Reno, NV 89557
Tel: 800-255-8343
http://www.judges.org

For information on the Supreme Court, such as recent rulings, contact
Supreme Court of the United States
http://www.supremecourtus.gov

Lawyers

QUICK FACTS

School Subjects
English
Government
Speech

Personal Skills
Communication/ideas
Leadership/management

Work Environment
Primarily indoors
Primarily multiple locations

Minimum Education Level
Law degree

Salary Range
$50,580 to $102,470 to
$1,000,000+

Certification or Licensing
Required

Outlook
About as fast as the average

DOT
110

GOE
11.04.02

NOC
4112

O*NET-SOC
23-1011.00

OVERVIEW

Lawyers, or *attorneys,* serve in two ways in our legal system: as advocates and as advisers. As advocates, they represent the rights of their clients in trials and depositions or in front of administrative and government bodies. As advisers, attorneys counsel clients on how the law affects business or personal decisions, such as the purchase of property or the creation of a will. Lawyers represent individuals, businesses, and corporations. Approximately 761,000 lawyers work in the United States today, in various areas of the profession.

HISTORY

The tradition of governing people by laws has been established over centuries. Societies have built up systems of law that have been studied and drawn upon by later governments. The earliest known law is the Code of Hammurabi, developed about 1800 B.C. by the ruler of the Sumerians. Another early set of laws was the Law of Moses, known as the Ten Commandments. Every set of laws, no matter when they were introduced, has been accompanied by the need for someone to explain those laws and help others live under them.

The great orators of ancient Greece and Rome set up schools for young boys to learn by apprenticeship the many skills involved in pleading a law case. To be an eloquent speaker was the greatest advantage. The legal profession has matured since those earlier times; a great deal of training and an extensive knowledge of legal matters are required of the modern lawyer.

Much modern European law was organized and refined by legal experts assembled by Napoleon; their body of law was known as the Napoleonic Code. English colonists coming to America brought English common law, from which American laws have grown. In areas of the United States that were heavily settled by Spanish colonists, there are traces of Spanish law. As the population in the country grew, along with business, those who knew the law were in high demand. The two main kinds of law are *civil* and *criminal,* but many other specialty areas are also prevalent today. When our country was young, most lawyers were general law practitioners—they knew and worked with all the laws for their clients' sakes. Today, there are many more lawyers who specialize in areas such as tax law, corporate law, and intellectual property law.

THE JOB

All lawyers may give legal advice and represent clients in court when necessary. No matter what their specialty, their job is to help clients know their rights under the law and then help them achieve these rights before a judge, jury, government agency, or other legal forum, such as an arbitration panel. Lawyers may represent businesses and individuals. For businesses, they manage tax matters, arrange for stock to be issued, handle claims cases, represent the firm in real estate dealings, and advise on all legal matters. For individuals they may be trustees, guardians, or executors; they may draw up wills or contracts or advise on income taxes or on the purchase or sale of a home. Some work solely in the courts; others carry on most of their business outside of court, doing such tasks as drawing up mortgages, deeds, contracts, and other legal documents or by handling the background work necessary for court cases, which might include researching cases in a law library or interviewing witnesses. A number of lawyers work to establish and enforce laws for the federal and state governments by drafting legislation, representing the government in court, or serving as judges.

Lawyers can also take positions as professors in law schools. Administrators, research workers, and writers are also important to the profession. Administrative positions in business or government may be of a nonlegal nature, but the qualities, background, and experience of a lawyer are often helpful in such positions.

Other individuals with legal training may choose not to practice but instead opt for careers in which their background and knowledge of law are important. These careers include *tax collectors, credit investigators, FBI agents, insurance adjusters, process servers,* and *probation officers.*

Some of the specialized fields for lawyers include the following:

Civil lawyers work in a field also known as private law. They focus on damage suits and breach-of-contract suits; prepare and draw up deeds, leases, wills, mortgages, and contracts; and act as trustees, guardians, or executors of an estate when necessary.

Criminal lawyers, also known as *defense lawyers,* specialize in cases dealing with offenses committed against society or the state, such as theft, murder, or arson. They interview clients and witnesses to ascertain facts in a case, correlate their findings with known cases, and prepare a case to defend a client against the charges made. They conduct a defense at the trial, examine witnesses, and summarize the case with a closing argument to a jury.

District attorneys, also known as *prosecuting attorneys,* represent the city, county, state, or federal government in court proceedings. They gather and analyze evidence and review legal material relevant to a lawsuit. Then they present their case to the grand jury, which decides whether the evidence is sufficient for an indictment. If it is not, the suit is dismissed and there is no trial. If the grand jury decides to indict the accused, however, the case goes to court, where the district attorney appears before the judge and jury to present evidence against the defendant.

Probate lawyers specialize in planning and settling estates. They draw up wills, deeds of trust, and similar documents for clients who want to plan for giving their belongings to their heirs when they die. Upon a client's death, probate lawyers vouch for the validity of the will and represent the executors and administrators of the estate.

Bankruptcy attorneys assist their clients, both individuals and corporations, in obtaining protection from creditors under existing bankruptcy laws and with financial reorganization and debt repayment.

Corporation lawyers, sometimes known as *corporate lawyers,* advise corporations concerning their legal rights, obligations, or privileges. They study constitutions, statutes, previous decisions, ordinances, and decisions of quasi-judicial bodies that are applicable to corporations. They advise corporations on the pros and cons of prosecuting or defending a lawsuit. They act as agent of the corporation in various transactions and seek to keep clients from expensive litigation.

Maritime lawyers, sometimes referred to as *admiralty lawyers,* specialize in laws regulating commerce and navigation on the high seas and any navigable waters, including inland lakes and rivers. Although there is a general maritime law, it operates in each country according to that country's courts, laws, and customs. Maritime law covers contracts, insurance, property damage, and personal injuries.

Intellectual property lawyers focus on helping their clients with patents, trademarks, and copyright protection. (See the article Intellectual Property Lawyers.) *Patent lawyers* are intellectual property lawyers who specialize in securing patents for inventors from the United States Patent Office and prosecuting or defending suits of patent infringements. They prepare detailed specifications for the patent, may organize a corporation, or advise an existing corporation to commercialize on a patent. (See the article Patent Lawyers.) Biotechnology patent law is a further specialization of patent law. *Biotechnology patent lawyers* specialize in helping biotechnology researchers, scientists, and research corporations with all legal aspects of their biotechnology patents.

Elder law attorneys are lawyers who specialize in providing legal services for the elderly and, in some cases, the disabled. (See the article Elder Law Attorneys.)

Tax attorneys handle cases resulting from problems of inheritance, income tax, estate tax, franchises, and real estate tax, among other things.

Insurance attorneys advise insurance companies about legal matters pertaining to insurance transactions. They approve the wording of insurance policies, review the legality of claims against the company, and draw up legal documents.

An *international lawyer* specializes in the body of rules that are observed by nations in their relations with one another. Some of these laws have been agreed to in treaties, some have evolved from long-standing customs and traditions.

Securities and exchange lawyers monitor individuals and corporations involved in trading and oversee their activities to make sure they comply with applicable laws. When corporations undergo takeovers and mergers, securities and exchange lawyers are there to represent the corporations' interests and fulfill all legal obligations involved in the transaction.

Real estate lawyers handle the transfer of property and perform such duties as searching public records and deeds to establish titles of property, holding funds for investment in escrow accounts, and acting as trustees of property. They draw up legal documents and act as agents in various real estate transactions.

Title attorneys deal with titles, leases, contracts, and other legal documents pertaining to the ownership of land, and gas, oil, and mineral rights. They prepare documents to cover the purchase or sale of such property and rights, examine documents to determine ownership, advise organizations about legal requirements concerning titles, and participate in the trial or lawsuits in connection with titles.

Other lawyers may specialize in environmental, employee benefits, entertainment, or health law.

It is important to note that once you are licensed to practice law, you are legally qualified to practice any one or more of these and many other specialties. Some general practitioners handle both criminal and civil matters of all sorts. To become licensed, you must be admitted to the bar of that state. *Bar examiners* test the qualifications of applicants. They prepare and administer written exams covering legal subjects, examine candidates orally, and recommend admission of those who meet the prescribed standards.

REQUIREMENTS

High School
A high school diploma, a college degree, and three years of law school are minimum requirements for a law degree. A high school diploma is a first step on the ladder of education that a lawyer must climb. If you are considering a career in law, courses such as government, history, social studies, and economics provide a solid background for entering college-level courses. Speech courses are also helpful to build strong communication skills necessary for the profession. Also take advantage of any computer-related classes or experience you can get, because lawyers often use technology to research and interpret the law, from surfing the Internet to searching legal databases.

Postsecondary Training
To enter any law school approved by the American Bar Association, you must satisfactorily complete at least three, and usually four, years of college work. Most law schools do not specify any particular courses for prelaw education. Usually a liberal arts track is most advisable, with courses in English, history, economics, social sciences, logic, and public speaking. A college student planning on specialization in a particular area of law, however, might also take courses significantly related to that area, such as economics, agriculture, or political science. Those interested should contact several law schools to learn more about any requirements and to see if they will accept credits from the college the student is planning to attend.

Currently, 195 law schools in the United States are approved by the American Bar Association; others, many of them night schools, are approved by state authorities only. Most of the approved law schools, however, do have night sessions to accommodate part-time students. Part-time courses of study usually take four years.

Law school training consists of required courses such as legal writing and research, contracts, criminal law, constitutional law, torts, and property. The second and third years may be devoted to specialized courses of interest to the student, such as evidence, business transactions and corporations, or admiralty. The study of cases and decisions is of basic importance to the law student, who will be required to read and study thousands of these cases. A degree of juris doctor (JD) or bachelor of laws (LLB) is usually granted upon graduation. Some law students considering specialization, research, or teaching may go on for advanced study.

Most law schools require that applicants take the Law School Admission Test (LSAT), where prospective law students are tested on their critical thinking, writing, and reasoning abilities.

Certification or Licensing
Every state requires that lawyers be admitted to the bar of that state before they can practice. They require that applicants graduate from an approved law school and that they pass a written examination in the state in which they intend to practice. In a few states, graduates of law schools within the state are excused from these written examinations. After lawyers have been admitted to the bar in one state, they can practice in another state without taking a written examination if the states have reciprocity agreements; however, they will be required to meet certain state standards of good character and legal experience and pay any applicable fees.

Other Requirements
Federal courts and agencies have their own rules regulating admission to practice. Other requirements vary among the states. For example, the states of Vermont, New York, Washington, Virginia, California, Maine, and Wyoming allow a person who has spent several years reading law in a law office but has no college training or who has a combination of reading and law school experience to take the state bar examination. Few people now enter law practice in this manner.

A few states accept the study of law by correspondence. Some states require that newly graduated lawyers serve a period of clerkship in an established law firm before they are eligible to take the bar examination.

Lawyers have to be effective communicators, work well with people, and be able to find creative solutions to problems, such as complex court cases.

EXPLORING
If a career as a lawyer is of interest you, there are several ways you can find out more about it before making that final decision. First,

Lawyers conduct research in their firm's library. (*Syracuse Newspapers, David Lassman, The Image Works*)

sit in on a trial or two at your local or state courthouse. Try to focus mainly on the lawyer and take note of what he or she does. Write down questions you have and terms or actions you do not understand. Then, talk to your guidance counselor and ask for help in setting up a telephone or in-person interview with a lawyer. Ask questions and get the scoop on what this career is all about. Also, talk to your guidance counselor or political science teacher about starting or joining a job-shadowing program. Job shadowing programs allow you to follow a person in a certain career around for a day or two to get an idea of what goes on in a typical day. You may even be invited to help out with a few minor duties.

You can also search the Internet for general information about lawyers and current court cases. After you have done some research and talked to a lawyer and you still think you are destined for law school, try to get a part-time job in a law office. Ask your guidance counselor for help.

If you are already in law school, you might consider becoming a student member of the American Bar Association. Student members receive *Student Lawyer,* a magazine that contains useful information for aspiring lawyers. Sample articles from the magazine can be read at http://www.abanet.org/lsd/studentlawyer.

EMPLOYERS

Approximately 761,000 lawyers are employed in the United States. About 75 percent of them work in private practice, either in law firms or alone. The others are employed in government, often at the local level. Lawyers working for the federal government hold positions in the Departments of Justice, Treasury, and Defense. Lawyers also hold positions as house counsel for public utilities, transportation companies, banks, insurance companies, real estate agencies, manufacturing firms, welfare and religious organizations, and other businesses and nonprofit organizations.

STARTING OUT

The first steps in entering the law profession are graduation from an approved law school and passing a state bar examination. Usually beginning lawyers do not go into solo practice right away. It is often difficult to become established, and additional experience is helpful to the beginning lawyer. Also, most lawyers do not specialize in a particular branch of law without first gaining experience. Beginning lawyers usually work as assistants to experienced lawyers. At first they do mainly research and routine work. After a few years of successful experience, they may be ready to go out on their own. Other choices open to the beginning lawyer include joining an established law firm

Diversity in the Legal Profession

Although the number of minorities in the legal profession has increased in recent years, they are still underrepresented in terms of their total percentage of the U.S. population, according to a survey of firms by the National Association for Law Placement. In fact:

- Only 5.4 percent of partners at law firms in 2007 were minorities.
- Only 18 percent of associates at law firms in 2007 were minorities. Asian/Pacific Islanders made up nearly 9 percent of associates; African Americans, 4.7 percent; and Hispanic Americans, 3.7 percent.
- In 2006, women made up 17.9 percent of partners, 44.3 percent of associates, and 34.1 percent of all other lawyers at law firms.

The American Bar Association offers a variety of resources and programs to advance diversity in the legal profession. Visit http://www.abanet.org/lawyer.html to learn more.

or entering into partnership with another lawyer. Positions are also available with banks, business corporations, insurance companies, private utilities, and with a number of government agencies at different levels.

Many new lawyers are recruited by law firms or other employers directly from law school. Recruiters come to the school and interview possible hires. Other new graduates can get job leads from local and state bar associations.

ADVANCEMENT

Lawyers with outstanding ability can expect to go a long way in their profession. Novice lawyers generally start as law clerks, but as they prove themselves and develop their abilities, many opportunities for advancement will arise. They may be promoted to junior partner in a law firm or establish their own practice. Lawyers may enter politics and become judges, mayors, congressmen, or other government leaders. Top positions are available in business, too, for the qualified lawyer. Lawyers working for the federal government advance according to the civil service system.

EARNINGS

Incomes generally increase as the lawyer gains experience and becomes better known in the field. The beginning lawyer in solo practice may barely make ends meet for the first few years. According to the National Association for Law Placement, 2005 median salaries for new lawyers were $60,000. Those working for the government made approximately $46,158. Starting salaries for lawyers in business were $60,000. Recent graduates entering private practice made the most, earning approximately $85,000.

Experienced lawyers earn salaries that vary depending on the type, size, and location of their employers. According to the U.S. Department of Labor, the 2006 median salary for practicing lawyers was $102,470, although some senior partners earned well over $1 million a year. Ten percent earned less than $50,580. General attorneys in the federal government received $116,700 in 2006. State and local government attorneys generally made less, earning $77,970 and $84,570, respectively, in 2006. Benefits include paid vacation, health, disability, life insurance, and retirement or pension plans.

WORK ENVIRONMENT

Offices and courtrooms are usually pleasant, although busy, places to work. Lawyers also spend significant amounts of time in law libraries or record rooms, in the homes and offices of clients, and sometimes in the jail cells of clients or prospective witnesses. Many lawyers never work in a courtroom. Unless they are directly involved in litigation, they may never perform at a trial.

Some courts, such as small claims, family, or surrogate, may have evening hours to provide flexibility to the community. Criminal arraignments may be held at any time of the day or night. Court hours for most lawyers are usually regular business hours, with a one-hour lunch break. Often lawyers have to work long hours, spending evenings and weekends preparing cases and materials and working with clients. In addition to the work, the lawyer must always keep up with the latest developments in the profession. Also, it takes a long time to become a qualified lawyer, and it may be difficult to earn an adequate living until the lawyer gets enough experience to develop an established private practice.

Lawyers who are employed at law firms must often work grueling hours to advance in the firm. Spending long weekend hours doing research and interviewing people should be expected.

OUTLOOK

According to the *Occupational Outlook Handbook,* employment for lawyers is expected to grow about as fast as the average for all occupations through 2016, but large numbers of law school graduates have created strong competition for jobs, even though the number of graduates has begun to level off. Continued population growth, typical business activities, and increased numbers of legal cases involving health care, antitrust, environmental, intellectual property, international law, venture capital, energy, elder law, and sexual harassment issues, among others, will create a steady demand for lawyers. Law services will be more accessible to the middle-income public with the popularity of prepaid legal services and clinics. However, stiff competition has and will continue to urge some lawyers to look outside the legal profession for employment. Administrative and managerial positions in real-estate companies, banks, insurance firms, and government agencies are typical areas where legal training is useful.

The top 10 percent of the graduating seniors of the country's best law schools will have more opportunities with well-known law firms and jobs on legal staffs of corporations, in government agencies, and in law schools in the next few decades. Lawyers in solo practice will find it hard to earn a living until their practice is fully established. The best opportunities exist in small towns or suburbs of large cities, where there is less competition and new lawyers can meet potential clients more easily.

Graduates with lower class rankings and from lesser-known schools may have difficulty in obtaining the most desirable positions.

FOR MORE INFORMATION

For information about law student services offered by the ABA, contact
American Bar Association (ABA)
321 North Clark Street
Chicago, IL 60610-4714
Tel: 800-285-2221
Email: askaba@abanet.org
http://www.abanet.org

For information on workshops and seminars, contact
Association of American Law Schools
1201 Connecticut Avenue, NW, Suite 800
Washington, DC 20036-2717
Tel: 202-296-8851
Email: aals@aals.org
http://www.aals.org

The FBA provides information for lawyers and judges involved in federal practice.
Federal Bar Association (FBA)
Student Services
2011 Crystal Drive, Suite 400
Arlington, VA 22202-3709
Tel: 703-682-7000
Email: fba@fedbar.org
http://fedbar.org

For information on choosing a law school, law careers, salaries, and alternative law careers, contact
National Association for Law Placement
1025 Connecticut Avenue, NW, Suite 1110
Washington, DC 20036-5413
Tel: 202-835-1001
Email: info@nalp.org
http://www.nalp.org

For information on state courts, contact
National Center for State Courts
2425 Wilson Boulevard, Suite 350
Arlington, VA 22201-3320
http://www.ncsconline.org

For information on the Supreme Court, such as recent rulings, contact
Supreme Court of the United States
http://www.supremecourtus.gov

Legal Nurse Consultants

QUICK FACTS

School Subjects
Biology
Chemistry

Personal Skills
Helping/teaching
Technical/scientific

Work Environment
Primarily indoors
Primarily multiple locations

Minimum Education Level
Some postsecondary
training

Salary Range
$30,000 to $45,000 to
$100,000+

Certification or Licensing
Voluntary

Outlook
Faster than the average

DOT
N/A

GOE
04.02.02, 14.02.01

NOC
N/A

O*NET-SOC
N/A

OVERVIEW

Legal nurse consultants are members of a litigation team that deals with medical malpractice, personal injury, and product liability lawsuits as well as other medically related legal cases. They may be employed independently on a contract or retainer basis; or they may be employed by a law firm, insurance company, corporation, government agency, or as part of a risk management department in a hospital. Legal nurse consultants are trained nurses who have a thorough understanding of medical issues and trends. They utilize their clinical experience, knowledge of health care standards, and medical resources to assist litigation teams and act as liaisons between the legal and health care communities. Their primary role is to evaluate, analyze, and render informed opinions regarding health care. They practice in both plaintiff and defense capacities in collaboration with attorneys and others involved in legal processes. The American Association of Legal Nurse Consultants has approximately 3,500 members.

HISTORY

Nurses have served as expert witnesses in nursing malpractice cases for many years. But it was not until the early 1970s, according to the American Association of Legal Nurse Consultants (AALNC), that nurses began to receive compensation for providing this much-needed expertise to the legal community. As nursing and medical malpractice litigation increased in the 1980s, more nurses were needed to serve as expert witnesses in legal proceedings. During this time, according to the AALNC, nurses also began assisting lawyers with understanding medical records and literature, hospital policies and procedures, and medical testimony. Law firms quickly realized that legal nurse consultants were a knowledgeable, cost-effective alternative to physician consultants and began to hire these professionals to assist them with not only nursing and medical malpractice issues, but also personal injury and criminal cases.

The American Association of Legal Nurse Consultants was founded in 1989 to serve the professional needs of legal nurse consultants. It has approximately 3,400 members.

THE JOB

Legal nurse consultants' job responsibilities vary depending on the case and its medical implications. When working on a case, they may conduct client interviews, which involves talking to persons who feel they have a legal claim against a medical facility or doctor or nurse, or as a result of an accident.

They may research past medical cases and treatments. They often advise attorneys regarding medical facts, treatments, and other medical issues that are relevant to a case. Legal nurse consultants obtain and organize medical records, and locate and procure evidence. They may identify, interview, and retain expert witnesses. They may also assist with depositions and trials, including developing and preparing exhibits for jury or judge trials.

As part of legal teams, legal nurse consultants are often required to do considerable research and paperwork. "As a legal nurse consultant," says Sherri Reed, BSN, RN, LNCC, and former president of the AALNC, "you must be totally responsible for your part of the job. If information is to be gathered and reports written, you need to get it done. There is no one to take over at shift change. It is entirely your responsibility and you can't pass it on to someone else."

Independent legal nurse consultants must also be responsible for getting their work done within a strict deadline. They often work under a contract and must produce the records, information, and reports within a specified time frame.

In addition, they must generate their own clients. This requires that they be business-minded and do their own marketing to the legal field. Independent legal nurse consultants need to learn and practice business skills such as marketing, sales, and record keeping.

"Nurses are nurturers by nature," says Reed. "Because of these predominant traits, many need to learn to be aggressive and assertive and be their own salespeople if they are going to find work."

Legal nurse consultants can expect their jobs to be demanding, but that is what Reed likes best about her job. "I like my independence and using my knowledge to analyze and research cases. It is challenging and stimulating. There are always new cases and issues."

REQUIREMENTS

High School

In high school, take mathematics and science courses, including biology, chemistry, and physics. Health courses will also be helpful. English and speech courses should not be neglected because you must be able to communicate well with lawyers and other legal professionals. Business and accounting classes will provide you with the basic tools necessary to run a business.

Postsecondary Training

Legal nurse consultants must first become registered nurses. "All legal nurse consultants must have clinical nursing experience," says Reed who is employed as a legal nurse consultant with an Indiana law firm. "This is extremely important since they need this work experience to draw on in order to present cases and testify. They must have up-to-date medical knowledge they can utilize."

Legal nurse consultants should have work experience in critical care areas such as hospital emergency rooms, intensive care units, and obstetrics, since these are the areas that are most likely to be involved in litigation. Legal education is not a prerequisite, although many legal nurse consultants acquire knowledge of the legal system by consulting with attorneys, taking classes, and attending seminars.

Many independent legal nurse consultants are practicing nurses. According to Reed, "It is important for legal nurse consultants to stay abreast of changes in the medical field. They need to actively practice nursing or take continuing education courses to stay current. They must be able to apply their knowledge and evaluate medical issues in litigation."

A few colleges (such as Bergen Community College, Elgin Community College, Kent State University, and Madonna University) offer associate degrees and advanced certificates in legal consulting.

Certification or Licensing

The legal nurse consultant certified (LNCC) program is the only certification in legal nurse consulting recognized by the American Association of Legal Nurse Consultants. Administered by the American Legal Nurse Consultant Certification Board, the LNCC program promotes the recognition of legal nurse consulting as a specialty practice of nursing. The certification, which is voluntary, is renewed every five years through continuing education or reexamination and continued practice in the specialty.

Other Requirements

To be a successful legal nurse consultant, you should enjoy organizing information and writing reports, be able to explain medical issues and procedures to people with nonmedical backgrounds, and be skilled to handle multiple tasks under deadline pressure. You should also have strong reasoning skills, self-motivation, and the ability to work well with many types of people.

If you also practice as a nurse, you should enjoy working with people and be able to give directions as well as follow instructions and work as part of a health care team. Anyone interested in becoming a registered nurse should also have a strong desire to continue learning because new tests, procedures, and technologies are constantly being developed for the medical world.

EXPLORING

You can learn more about nursing and legal issues by visiting the Web sites of nursing and legal associations, reading books or magazines (such as the *Journal of Legal Nurse Consulting,* which is available from the AALNC) on the subjects, or conducting an information interview with a registered nurse, a legal nurse consultant, or a lawyer who specializes in health care issues. You might also visit hospitals to observe the work and to talk with hospital personnel.

Some hospitals now have extensive volunteer service programs in which students can work after school, on weekends, or during vacations. You can find other volunteer work experiences with the Red Cross or community health services.

To learn more about the legal aspects of legal nurse consulting, you might consider trying to get an internship at a law firm that specializes in health care law.

EMPLOYERS

Legal nurse consultants may be employed independently on a contract or retainer basis, or they may be employed by a law firm, insurance company, corporation, or government agency, or as part of a risk management department in a hospital.

STARTING OUT

The only way to become a registered nurse is through completion of one of the three kinds of educational programs plus passing the licensing examination. Registered nurses may apply for employment directly to hospitals, nursing homes, and companies and government agencies that hire nurses. Jobs can also be obtained through school career services offices, by signing up with employment agencies specializing in placement of nursing personnel, or through the state employment office. Other sources of jobs include nurses' associations, professional journals, and newspaper want ads.

ADVANCEMENT

Administrative and supervisory positions in the nursing field go to nurses who have earned at least the bachelor of science degree in nursing. Nurses with many years of experience who are graduates of the diploma program may achieve supervisory positions, but requirements for such promotions have become more difficult in recent years and in many cases require at least the bachelor of science in nursing degree.

Legal nurse consultants with considerable experience may advance to supervisory positions or move on to open their own consulting companies.

EARNINGS

Persons who work as independent legal nurse consultants are usually paid on an hourly basis that can range from $60 to $250 per hour. The fee depends on the type of services they are performing, such as testifying, reviewing records, or doing medical research the fee also reflects their experience and reputation. In addition, fees vary in different parts of the country. Some legal nurse consultants may work on a retainer basis with one or more clients.

Many legal nurse consultants who work for law firms and other businesses and institutions are employed full or part time. Their salaries vary by experience, geographic location, and areas of expertise. The full-time salary range is from under $30,000 to a small percentage making more than $100,000. Some litigation situations may require that consultants work overtime.

General employment benefits such as health and life insurance, vacation time, and sick leave may be offered to full-time legal nurse consultants.

WORK ENVIRONMENT

Working environments may vary depending on the consultants' responsibilities and their legal cases. According to a survey conducted by AALNC, 53 percent of legal nurse consultants were in independent practice, and law firms employed 32 percent. Office environments where consultants work are usually clean and well lighted. However, research and interview requirements may take consultants to communities that range from safe to less than desirable.

OUTLOOK

Nursing specialties will be in great demand in the future. The U.S. Department of Labor reports that employment of registered nurses will grow much faster than the average for all occupations through 2016.

The outlook for legal nurse consultants is excellent. According to Sherri Reed, "It is an up-and-coming profession. Our association [AALNC] has grown rapidly and we hope to increase the profession's visibility."

FOR MORE INFORMATION

For information on educational opportunities in nursing, contact
American Association of Colleges of Nursing
One Dupont Circle, NW, Suite 530
Washington, DC 20036-1135
Tel: 202-463-6930
http://www.aacn.nche.edu

For information on certification and to read Getting Started in Legal Nurse Consulting: An Introduction to the Specialty, *visit the AALNC's Web site.*
American Association of Legal Nurse Consultants (AALNC)
401 North Michigan Avenue
Chicago, IL 60611-4255
Tel: 877-402-2562
Email: info@aalnc.org
http://www.aalnc.org

Legal Secretaries

QUICK FACTS

School Subjects
English
Government
Journalism

Personal Skills
Communication/ideas
Following instructions

Work Environment
Primarily indoors
Primarily one location

Minimum Education Level
Some postsecondary training

Salary Range
$23,870 to $38,190 to
$58,770+

Certification or Licensing
Recommended

Outlook
About as fast as the average

DOT
201

GOE
09.02.02

NOC
1242

O*NET-SOC
43-6012.00

OVERVIEW

Legal secretaries, sometimes called *litigation secretaries* or *trial secretaries*, assist lawyers by performing the administrative and clerical duties in a law office or firm. Legal secretaries spend most of their time writing legal correspondence, preparing legal documents, performing research, and answering incoming calls and emails. Legal secretaries read and review many law journals to check for any new court decisions that may be important for cases pending at that time. Legal secretaries also maintain files and records, take notes during meetings or hearings, and assume all other general secretarial duties. Approximately 275,000 legal secretaries work in law offices and firms in the United States today.

HISTORY

Over the years, the law has become increasingly complex. Along with that fact, more and more litigation proceedings have occurred which have led to the need for lawyers, first, to explain the law, and second, to pursue its defense. Originally, lawyers hired secretaries for their small, one- or two-lawyer office to assist with general clerical duties. Typing letters, filing documents, and receiving clients were the main duties of these general secretaries. As lawyers were forced to spend more of their time dealing with the difficulties of the law and with their increased number of clientele, secretaries were given more responsibility. The secretaries were transformed from being mainly receptionists to managing the law office, at least the administrative side of it. Lawyers started to look to their secretaries more as legal assistants than receptionists.

Today legal secretaries are indispensable to most lawyers and play a major role in each client's case by streamlining all documentation, communication, and research into a usable source of information.

The legal secretary field has also grown in this computer age. "As an example of how information technology has transformed the profession, 20 years ago the rule was 'one lawyer, one secretary,'" says professional legal secretary Alexis Montgomery. "Now with computer word processing, specialized programs for legal practices, and information technology in all of its forms, typically one experienced legal secretary can handle two lawyers." Although most computer advances have helped the legal secretary field expand, some lawyers are using this technology to increase their own productivity. The lawyer can reassume some duties that the legal secretary does now—reducing the need for secretaries.

Although lawyers may be more computer-savvy, legal secretaries still play an important, but changing role. For example, whereas before the legal secretary took dictation, typed out a letter, and then proofread it for accuracy, now the lawyer may type his own letter on the computer and ask the legal secretary to edit it and to fact check some of the main points. Lawyers aren't the only ones taking advantage of new technology; legal secretaries now have the advantage of using personal computers instead of electronic typewriters, and fax machines instead of telex machines. The World Wide Web has made research much easier as well.

THE JOB

Legal secretaries must be able to handle all the duties of a general secretary plus all the specific responsibilities that come with working for a lawyer. Although every law office or firm may vary in the exact duties required for the position, in general, most legal secretaries spend their time managing information that comes in and goes out of the law office. "No one day is the same with my job," says Julie Abernathy, a legal secretary at Haynes and Boone, L.L.P. in Austin, Texas. "That in itself is what I love most about my career. Each case is different from the next, and each client is unique in their/its own way. I typically interact with the clients, prepare correspondence, transmitting pleadings and documents to opposing counsel, court house personnel, and clients for review and approval. My supervising attorneys do not give me specific instructions, as they know I am very familiar with procedures and responsibilities with my job. I also assist my attorneys with basic research, document retrieval, document production, and even with their travel arrangements."

Legal secretaries may type letters and legal documents, such as subpoenas, appeals, and motions; handle incoming and outgoing mail; maintain a detailed filing system; and deliver legal documents to the court. Besides these duties, legal secretaries spend much of their time making appointments with clients, and dealing with client questions. "An important part of being an effective legal secretary is fielding telephone calls and all client contact efficiently and courteously," says Alexis Montgomery. "Often the client's primary contact is with the legal secretary and client satisfaction depends heavily on how helpful and courteous that contact is perceived." The legal secretary is a sort of personal assistant to one or more lawyers as well, and must maintain the calendars and schedules for the office. "Always knowing where your attorney can be found or whether another attorney can assist the client is an important part of the process," says Montgomery.

Legal secretaries are also called upon to conduct research for the cases that are current within the office. They may research and write legal briefs on a topic or case that is relevant to the lawyer's current cases. According to Rebecca Garland, a legal advocate who was trained as a legal secretary but is now using those skills to assist victims of domestic violence in obtaining personal protection orders, research often takes up an entire workday. "You may spend one whole day working on a legal brief for one client, and then spend the next day working on small things for several different cases." Legal secretaries spend many hours researching cases in law libraries, public libraries, and on the Internet. Part of this research includes scouring legal journals and magazines looking for relevant laws and courtroom decisions that may affect the clientele.

Legal secretaries are also record keepers. They help lawyers find information such as employment, medical, and criminal records. They also keep records from all previous clients and court cases for future use. Legal secretaries must also track and use various forms, such as trial request, client application, and accident report forms. "The bottom line is that legal secretaries process the paperwork generated by their attorneys," says Alexis Montgomery.

REQUIREMENTS

High School

Because a legal secretary must be able to communicate the attorney's ideas in written and oral form, it's important to get a firm grounding in English (especially writing), spelling, typing, and public speaking. Computers are used in most law offices, so be sure to gain computer experience while in high school. Government and political science courses will get you started on the road to legal knowledge as well. Classes that give you experience with research are also important. Rebecca Garland says, "Learning how to do research in the school or community library will go a long way in learning how to do research in a law library."

Postsecondary Training

Many legal secretaries get their training through established one- or two-year legal secretary programs. These programs are available at most business, vocational, and junior colleges. You could also obtain a four-year degree to get a more well-rounded education. Courses taken should focus on specific skills and knowledge needed by a legal secretary, such as personal computers, keyboarding, English, legal writing, editing, researching, and communication. NALS, the Association for Legal Professionals, also offers basic and advanced legal secretary training courses. (See their contact information at the end of this article.)

As businesses continue to expand worldwide, employers are increasingly looking for candidates with bachelor's degrees and professional certifications.

Certification or Licensing

Two general legal secretary certifications are offered by NALS, the Association for Legal Professionals. After some preliminary office training, you can take an examination to receive the accredited legal secretary designation. This certification is for legal secretaries with education, but little to no experience. Legal secretaries with three years of experience can become certified as a professional legal secretary (PLS). The PLS certification designates a legal secretary with exceptional skills and experience.

Other specific legal secretary certifications are given by Legal Secretaries International. You can become board certified in civil litigation, probate, real estate, business law, criminal law, or intellectual property. Applicants must have a minimum of five years of law experience and pass an examination.

Other Requirements

To be employed as a legal secretary, you must learn a great deal of legal terminology and court structures and practices. Whether through study or experience, you must be able to grasp the inner workings of the law. "Excellent grammar and composition skills are two of the most important attributes needed for this profession," advises Patricia Infanti, a legal secretary for more than 30 years. In addition, you must also be able to quickly learn computer programs,

The Pros and Cons of Being a Legal Secretary

The editors of *Careers in Focus: Law* asked Julie Abernathy, a legal secretary at Haynes and Boone, LLP, what she likes most and least about her job. The following are her comments:

I love interacting with the clients. I also enjoy organizing a case either in hard copies or electronically on our databases here at the firm. Often times our clients have access to our databases through the Internet, therefore, it is imperative that I maintain everything for their immediate accessibility.

Another thing I love about my job is my membership in NALS. It was my first employer's suggestion that I join the local chapter in Waco. I have been a member of NALS since 1975. Without the continuing education, networking, certifications, and basic overall leadership skills that I have learned and obtained through NALS, I would not be the person I am today. Legal skills are continual. You do not learn it all in school. What you learn in school are the basics, but it is the "hands on" experiences with the real world that teach you most.

As with most clerical jobs, the least favorite would have to be filing. However, filing is probably one of most important aspects of my job. If you can't find it, you're lost. My attorneys expect immediate accessibility to all documents and communications on each case.

especially word processing and database programs, and be able to use them skillfully. "Students interested in this career need to know their way around the keyboard," says Infanti. "They should also know basic and advanced applications in Microsoft Word, Outlook, Excel, and PowerPoint." The ability to prioritize and balance different tasks is also necessary for the job. Legal secretaries must be organized and focused to handle their varying responsibilities.

EXPLORING

Does a career as a legal secretary sound interesting? If so, suggest a career day at your school (if one isn't already scheduled) where professionals from a variety of careers give presentations. Be sure to let your career counselor know that you would like to have a legal secretary come as a guest speaker. Or you can ask your political science or government teacher to take your class on a field trip to a law library. Many law offices hire "runners" to deliver and file documents. Check with local law offices and offer your services for the summer or after school. You may also find it helpful to contact a local law firm and ask a legal secretary there if you can conduct an information interview.

EMPLOYERS

Approximately 275,000 legal secretaries are employed in the United States. The majority of legal secretaries work for law offices or law firms. Some government agencies on the state and national level also employ legal secretaries. More law firms and offices are located in Washington, D.C., and in larger metropolitan areas, so these regions offer more opportunities. However, most law offices and firms do business online. The Internet enables workers to send information easily from the law office to the courtroom, so offices are not forced to be located close to the courts. Legal secretaries are in demand anywhere lawyers practice.

STARTING OUT

Many legal secretaries get their first job through the career services offices of their college or vocational school. Still other legal secretaries start by working part-time, gaining experience toward a first full-time position. Alexis Montgomery started out that way: "My first employment was as a staff secretary on a newspaper. Thereafter I worked as a 'floater' in a medium-sized law firm. [A *floater* is a secretary who is not assigned to any particular lawyer, but fills in for absent secretaries and handles overflow.] This job was my first exposure to the field and provided on-the-job training as a legal secretary." Montgomery also adds that working as a floater exposes you to a wide variety of legal practices—useful when deciding which area you want to specialize in. Don't forget to contact the local law offices in your area and let them know you are available; often direct contact now can lead to a job later.

ADVANCEMENT

Experienced legal secretaries are often promoted to oversee less experienced legal secretaries. Some firms have senior legal secretaries who are given more responsibility and less supervision duties. "In many cases more experienced legal secretaries do the drafting of letters and documents and pass them on to the attorney for revision or signature," says Montgomery. "As one becomes more experienced and proficient, the work of a legal secretary tends to blend into what is regarded as paralegal work." Legal secretaries may continue their education and become paralegals themselves. Many of the skills legal secretaries obtain can be transferred to almost any other office setting.

EARNINGS

According to the U.S. Department of Labor, the average salary for legal secretaries was approximately $38,190 in 2006. Salaries ranged from less than $23,870 to more than $58,770. An attorney's rank in the firm will also affect the salary of his or her legal secretary; secretaries who work for a partner will earn higher salaries than those who work for an associate. Certified legal secretaries generally receive higher pay.

Most law firms provide employees with sick days, vacation days, and holidays. Health insurance, 401(k) plans, and profit sharing may be offered as well. Some law firms offer in-house training or pay for off-site classes to increase their secretarial skills.

WORK ENVIRONMENT

Legal secretaries spend the majority of their day behind their desk at a computer. They spend lengthy periods of time typing or writing, which may cause hand and wrist strain. Long hours staring at a computer monitor may also cause eyestrain. Legal secretaries work with lawyers, other legal secretaries, clients, court personnel, library personnel, and other support workers. Senior legal secretaries supervise some legal secretaries; others are left largely unsupervised. Most legal secretaries are full-time employees who work a 40-hour week. Some are part-time workers who move into full-time status as they gain more experience. Because the legal secretary's work revolves around the lawyer, many secretaries work long hours of overtime.

Legal secretaries may work at small, single attorney firms, mid-sized firms, or large law firms with offices throughout the United States. Patricia Infanti works at Ballard Spahr Andrews & Ingersoll, LLP, a large law firm with 10 offices. "Working for a large firm is a wonderful opportunity because large firms offer so many benefits and services that a small law firm simply cannot afford," she explains. "Not only is my work space well laid out with a large wrap-around desk and comfortable chair, but my printer is next to my desk and other office machines are close by. When I have computer difficulties, I have an entire department available to immediately assist me. In addition, there is a print room, mail room, and other services, which enable me to concentrate on my attorneys' work."

OUTLOOK

Because the legal services industry as a whole is growing, legal secretaries will be in demand. An increased need for lawyers in such areas as intellectual property cases will leave lawyers in need of assistance with their caseloads. Qualified legal secretaries will have plentiful job opportunities, especially in the larger metropolitan areas.

Technological advances in recent years have revolutionized traditional secretarial tasks such as typing or keeping correspondence. The use of email, scanners, and the Internet will make secretaries more productive in coming years. The downside to these advancements is a possible decrease in demand: Fewer workers are needed to do the same workload. For the legal profession, however, advances in technology have only expanded the responsibilities for secretaries. According to the *Occupational Outlook Handbook,* employment for legal secretaries will grow about as fast as the average for all occupations through 2016. "The role of 'legal secretary' may change throughout the years, but it will never phase out," predicts Julie Abernathy. "I can only imagine what my job will be like in the next 10 to 15 years and am looking forward to learning new things."

FOR MORE INFORMATION

For information about certification, careers, and job listings, contact
Legal Secretaries International
2302 Fannin Street, Suite 500
Houston, TX 77002-9136
http://www.legalsecretaries.org

For information on certification, job openings, a variety of careers in law, and more, contact
NALS...the association for legal professionals
314 East 3rd Street, Suite 210
Tulsa, OK 74120-2409
Tel: 918-582-5188
Email: info@nals.org
http://www.nals.org

INTERVIEW

Dee Beardsley is a legal secretary supervisor at Latham & Watkins LLP in San Diego, California. She is also the president-elect of NALS, the Association for Legal Professionals. Dee discussed her career with the editors of Careers in Focus: Law.

Q. How long have you been a legal secretary? Please tell us briefly about your firm.

A. I began my career as a legal secretary in 1975. I also worked as a corporate paralegal for many years. I have been at my current firm for 20 years (as a legal secretary) and became the legal secretary supervisor in the San Diego office in October 2006.

Latham & Watkins LLP was founded in 1934 in Los Angeles, California, and has grown into a full-service international firm with more than 2,100 attorneys in 27 offices around the world. The firm is ranked fourth on The American Lawyer's A-List and was selected as the "Law Firm of the Decade" in the *Legal Business* 2007 awards. It has also received numerous international awards in all practice areas.

Q. Why did you decide to become a legal secretary?

A. During the recession in the mid-70s I was overeducated and underqualified for many positions. My father was a patent lawyer and always held his legal secretary in the highest regard. I went back to school to learn the skills necessary to work in a law firm and was hired before I graduated. I obtained my professional legal secretary certification in 1984 and later my professional paralegal certification.

Being a legal secretary has been absolutely the best career choice for me. There is never a dull moment. It has enabled me to work with brilliant, well-educated, dynamic professionals who care about—and make a difference in—the world. I have worked in the family law, environmental, labor, real estate, estate planning, corporate, and business fields. I have worked in law offices in Germany and Belgium.

Q. What is the biggest misconception about legal secretaries?

A. That they are "just" secretaries. It's not about the title; it's about the work. Legal secretaries are multi-taskers, problem solvers, researchers, and gatekeepers. They are service-oriented, intellectually curious, and dedicated professionals.

Q. What type of educational path did you pursue to become a legal secretary?

A. I hold a bachelor's degree in English and completed post-graduate work in telecommunications and film. I graduated with honors from the legal studies program at a local business school, which taught legal, executive, and medical curricula.

Q. **What advice would you give to high school students who are interested in this career?**

A. Follow your passion and cultivate your extracurricular interests; whatever they are, there is a corresponding field of law you can specialize in if you choose. Develop your research skills and pursue your intellectual curiosity about the world. Learn business software (Word, Excel, PowerPoint) and throw in a psychology course or two; you will encounter a wide variety of people in your career, and knowing something about what makes them tick will make your life a lot easier! NALS, the association for legal professionals, offers student memberships and opportunities for networking and continuing legal education through its Online Learning Center. Visit http://www.nals.org to learn more.

Q. **What is the future employment outlook in the field?**

A. Historically, the demand for good legal secretaries has always been high. In times of recession, and even during the Great Depression, legal secretaries always worked. It is a portable career that can move with you across the country and around the world, and one that is not limited to law firms. Legal secretaries possess skills that are transferable to the corporate world and nonprofit arena as well.

Paralegals

QUICK FACTS

School Subjects
Computer science
English
Government

Personal Skills
Communication/ideas
Following instructions

Work Environment
Primarily indoors
Primarily multiple locations

Minimum Education Level
Some postsecondary training

Salary Range
$27,450 to $43,040 to
$67,540+

Certification or Licensing
Voluntary

Outlook
Much faster than the average

DOT
119

GOE
04.04.02

NOC
4211

O*NET-SOC
23-2011.00

OVERVIEW

Paralegals, also known as *legal assistants*, assist in trial preparations, investigate facts, prepare documents such as affidavits and pleadings, and, in general, do work customarily performed by lawyers. Approximately 238,000 paralegals and legal assistants work in law firms, businesses, and government agencies all over the United States; the majority work with lawyers and legislators.

HISTORY

The U.S. legal system has undergone many changes over the past few decades as more people turn to lawyers for help in settling disputes. This increase in litigation has placed greater demands on lawyers and other legal professionals. To help meet these demands, lawyers have hired legal assistants to help provide legal services to more people at a lower cost.

The first paralegals were given a limited number of routine duties. Many started as legal secretaries who were gradually given more responsibilities. Today, however, the work of the paralegal has expanded and formal training programs have been established.

Since this occupation developed in the late 1960s, paralegals have taken on much of the routine work that lawyers once did, such as researching, investigating, and preparing legal briefs. Their work allows lawyers to concentrate on the more technical aspects of providing legal services. The paralegal profession continues to grow as they gain wider acceptance as legal professionals.

Computers play an important role in the research conducted by paralegals today. A paralegal must be proficient at using the computer to find information and to create reports.

THE JOB

A paralegal's main duty is to do everything a lawyer needs to do but does not have time to do. Although the lawyer assumes responsibility for the paralegal's work, the paralegal may take on all the duties of the lawyer except for setting fees, appearing in court, accepting cases, and giving legal advice.

Paralegals spend much of their time in law libraries, researching laws and previous cases and compiling facts to help lawyers prepare for trial. Paralegals often interview witnesses as part of their research as well. After analyzing the laws and facts that have been compiled for a particular client, the paralegal often writes a report that the lawyer may use to determine how to proceed with the case. If a case is brought to trial, the paralegal helps prepare legal arguments and draft pleadings to be filed in court. They also organize and store files and correspondence related to cases.

Not all paralegal work centers on trials. Many paralegals work for corporations, agencies, schools, and financial institutions. *Corporate paralegals* create and maintain contracts, mortgages, affidavits, and other documents. They assist with corporate matters, such as shareholder agreements, contracts, and employee benefit plans. Another important part of a corporate paralegal's job is to stay on top of new laws and regulations to make sure the company is operating within those parameters.

Some paralegals work for the government. They may prepare complaints or talk to employers to find out why health or safety standards are not being met. They often analyze legal documents, collect evidence for hearings, and prepare explanatory material on various laws for use by the public. For example, a *court administrator paralegal* is in charge of keeping the courthouse functioning; tasks include monitoring personnel, handling the case load for the court, and general administration.

Other paralegals are involved in community or public-service work. They may help specific groups, such as poor or elderly members of the community. They may file forms, research laws, and prepare documents. They may represent clients at hearings, although they may not appear in court on behalf of a client.

Many paralegals work for large law firms, agencies, and corporations and specialize in a particular area of law. Some work for smaller firms and have a general knowledge of many areas of law. Paralegals have varied duties, and an increasing number use computers in their work.

REQUIREMENTS

High School
While in high school, take a broad range of subjects, including English, social studies or government, computer science, and languages, especially Spanish and Latin. Because legal terminology is used constantly, word origins and vocabulary should be a focus.

Postsecondary Training
Requirements for paralegals vary by employer. Some paralegals start out as legal secretaries or clerical workers and gradually are given more training and responsibility. The majority, however, choose formal training and education programs.

Formal training programs usually range from one to three years and are offered in a variety of educational settings: four-year colleges and universities, law schools, community and junior colleges, business schools, proprietary schools, and paralegal associations. Admission requirements vary, but good grades in high school and college are always an asset. There are approximately 1,000 paralegal programs, about 260 of which have been approved by the American Bar Association. The National Federation of Paralegal Associations reports that 84 percent of all paralegals receive formal paralegal education.

Some paralegal programs require a bachelor's degree for admission; others do not require any college education. In either case, those who have a college degree usually have an edge over those who do not.

Certification or Licensing
Paralegals are not required to be licensed or certified. Instead, when lawyers employ paralegals, they often follow guidelines designed to protect the public from the practice of law by unqualified persons.

Paralegals may, however, opt to be certified. To do so, they may take and pass an extensive two-day test conducted by the National Association of Legal Assistants (NALA) Certifying Board. Paralegals who pass the test may use the title certified legal assistant (CLA) after their names. CLAs who prefer to be referred to as "certified paralegals" can use the certified paralegal designation. The NALA also offers an advanced certified paralegal designation to experienced paralegals who complete education requirements. Several specialized courses are available, including Contracts Management/ Contracts Administration, Discovery, Social Security Disability, and Trial Practice. NALS, the Association for Legal Professionals, offers a basic and an advanced certification for legal professionals and the professional paralegal certification for paralegals. Contact the association for more information.

In 1994, the National Federation of Paralegal Associations established the Paralegal Advanced Competency Exam as a means for paralegals who fill education and experience requirements to acquire professional recognition. Paralegals who pass this exam and maintain the continuing education requirement may use the designation registered paralegal.

The American Alliance of Paralegals offers the American Alliance certified paralegal designation to applicants who have least five years of experience as a paralegal and meet educational criteria.

Other Requirements

Good communication skills, both verbal and written, are vital to working as a paralegal. You must be able to turn research into reports that a lawyer or corporate executive can use. You must also be able to think logically and learn new laws and regulations quickly. Research skills, computer skills, and people skills are other necessities.

EXPLORING

If you are interested in a career as a paralegal, but are unsure about it, do not worry. There are several ways you can explore the career of a paralegal. Colleges, universities, and technical schools have a wealth of information available for the asking. Elizabeth Houser, a practicing paralegal, recommends contacting schools that have paralegal programs directly. "Ask questions. They are helpful and will give you a lot of information about being a paralegal," she says.

Look for summer or part-time employment as a secretary or in the mailroom of a law firm to get an idea of the nature of the work. If paid positions are not available, volunteer in a nearby law office. Ask your guidance counselor to help you set up a volunteer/internship agreement with a lawyer.

Talk to your history or government teacher about organizing a trip to a lawyer's office and a courthouse. Ask your teacher to set aside time for you to talk to paralegals working there and to their supervising attorneys.

If you have access to a computer, search the World Wide Web for information on student organizations that are affiliated with the legal profession. You can also contact the organizations listed at the end of this article for general information.

EMPLOYERS

Paralegals and legal assistants hold approximately 238,000 jobs in the United States. The majority (70 percent) work for lawyers in law offices or in law firms. Other paralegals work for the government, namely for the Federal Trade Commission, Justice Department, Treasury Department, Internal Revenue Service, Department of the Interior, and many other agencies and offices. Paralegals also work in the business community. Anywhere legal matters are part of the day-to-day work, paralegals are usually handling them. Paralegals fit in well in business because many smaller corporations must deal with legal regulations but don't necessarily need an attorney or a team of lawyers.

Paralegals in business can be found all over the country. Larger cities employ more paralegals who focus on the legal side of the profession, and government paralegals will find the most opportunities in state capitals and Washington, D.C.

STARTING OUT

Although some law firms promote legal secretaries to paralegal status, most employers prefer to hire individuals who have completed paralegal programs. To have the best opportunity at getting a quality job in the paralegal field, you should attend a paralegal school. In addition to providing a solid background in paralegal studies, most schools help graduates find jobs. Even though the job market for paralegals is expected to grow rapidly over the next 10 years, those with the best credentials will get the best jobs.

For Elizabeth Houser, the internship program was the springboard to her first paralegal position. "The paralegal program of study I took required an internship. I was hired directly from that internship experience."

The National Federation of Paralegal Associations recommends using job banks that are sponsored by paralegal associations across the country. For paralegal associations that may be able to help, see the addresses listed at the end of this article. Many jobs for paralegals are posted on the Internet as well.

ADVANCEMENT

There are no formal advancement paths for paralegals. There are, however, some possibilities for advancement, as large firms are beginning to establish career programs for paralegals.

For example, a person may be promoted from a paralegal to a head legal assistant who supervises others. In addition, a paralegal may specialize in one area of law, such as environmental, real estate, or medical malpractice. Many paralegals also advance by moving from small to large firms.

Expert paralegals who specialize in one area of law may go into business for themselves. Rather than work for one firm, these freelance paralegals often contract their services to many lawyers. Some paralegals with bachelor's degrees enroll in law school to train to become lawyers.

Paralegals can also move horizontally by taking their specialized knowledge of the law into another field, such as insurance, occupational health, or law enforcement.

EARNINGS

Salaries vary greatly for paralegals. The size and location of the firm and the education and experience of the employee are some factors that determine the annual earnings of paralegals.

The U.S. Department of Labor (USDL) reports that paralegals and legal assistants had median annual earnings of $43,040 in 2006. The highest 10 percent earned more than $67,540, while the lowest 10 percent earned less than $27,450. According to the USDL, paralegals and legal assistants earned the following mean annual salaries in 2006 by industry: federal government, $57,590; local government, $44,580; legal services, $43,950; and state government, $40,870.

Benefits for paralegals depend on the employer; however, they usually include such items as health insurance, retirement or 401(k) plans, and paid vacation days.

WORK ENVIRONMENT

Paralegals often work in pleasant and comfortable offices. Much of their work is performed in a law library. Some paralegals work out of their homes in special employment situations. When investigation is called for, paralegals may travel to gather information. Most paralegals work a 40-hour week, although long hours are sometimes required to meet court-imposed deadlines. Longer hours—sometimes as much as 90 hours per week—are usually the normal routine for paralegals starting out in law offices and firms.

Many of the paralegal's duties involve routine tasks, so they must have a great deal of patience. However, paralegals may be given increasingly difficult assignments over time. Paralegals are often unsupervised, especially as they gain experience and a reputation for quality work. Elizabeth Houser does much of her work unsupervised. "You get to put a lot of yourself into what you do and that provides a high level of job satisfaction," she says.

OUTLOOK

Employment for paralegals is expected to grow much faster than the average for all occupations through 2016, according to the U.S. Department of Labor. One reason for the expected rapid growth in the profession is the financial benefits of employing paralegals. The paralegal, whose duties fall between those of the legal secretary and those of the attorney, helps make the delivery of legal services more cost effective to clients. The growing need for legal services among the general population and the increasing popularity of prepaid legal plans is creating a tremendous demand for paralegals in private law firms. In the private sector, paralegals can work in banks, insurance companies, real estate and title insurance firms, and corporate legal departments. In the public sector, there is a growing need for paralegals in the courts and community legal service programs, government agencies, and consumer organizations.

The growth of this occupation, to some extent, is dependent on the economy. Businesses are less likely to pursue litigation cases when profit margins are down, thus curbing the need for new hires.

FOR MORE INFORMATION

For information on certification, contact
American Alliance of Paralegals
16815 East Shea Boulevard, Suite 110, No. 101
Fountain Hills, AZ, 85268-6667
http://www.aapipara.org

For information regarding accredited educational facilities, contact
American Association for Paralegal Education
19 Mantua Road
Mt. Royal, NJ 08061-1006

Tel: 856-423-2829
Email: info@aafpe.org
http://www.aafpe.org

For general information about careers in the law field, contact
American Bar Association
Standing Committee on Paralegals
321 North Clark Street
Chicago, IL 60610-7598
Tel: 800-285-2221
http://www.abanet.org/legalservices/paralegals

For career information, contact
Association of Legal Administrators
75 Tri-State International, Suite 222
Lincolnshire, IL 60069-4435
Tel: 847-267-1252
http://www.alanet.org

For information on certification and careers in law, contact
NALS...the association for legal professionals
314 East 3rd Street, Suite 210
Tulsa, OK 74120-2409
Tel: 918-582-5188
Email: info@nals.org
http://www.nals.org

*For information about educational and licensing programs, certifi-
cation, and paralegal careers, contact*
National Association of Legal Assistants
1516 South Boston Avenue, Suite 200
Tulsa, OK 74119-4013
Tel: 918-587-6828
Email: nalanet@nala.org
http://www.nala.org

*For information about almost every aspect of becoming a paralegal,
contact*
National Federation of Paralegal Associations
PO Box 2016
Edmonds, WA 98020-9516
Tel: 425-967-0045
Email: info@paralegals.org
http://www.paralegals.org

For information about employment networks and school listings, contact

National Paralegal Association
PO Box 406
Solebury, PA 18963-0406
Tel: 215-297-8333
Email: admin@nationalparalegal.org
http://www.nationalparalegal.org

INTERVIEW

Kathy Siroky is a paralegal at Davis & Cannon, LLP, Attorneys at Law in Sheridan, Wyoming. She also recently served as the president of the NALS, the Association for Legal Professionals. Kathy discussed her career with the editors of Careers in Focus: Law.

Q. How long have you been a paralegal? Why did you decide to become a paralegal?

A. I have been a paralegal since 1998, beginning my career in the legal field quite by accident. After getting married and moving to a new town, I was unable to find employment in the school system and took a job as a legal secretary for a small law firm. I was very intrigued by the legal field and wanted to learn more and more. With my education and training came more responsibility and with that added responsibility came the title of paralegal. I wanted to use my knowledge and experience to help others.

Q. What do you like most and least about your job?

A. The most rewarding part of my job is the ability to help others when in need. My expertise is in the probate, business organization, and real estate fields. Clients come in at the most trying times of their lives—a loved one has passed away or they need help with a real estate problem—and I get to help them through all of the obstacles and have everything settled. Often a client send a note of thanks and it makes all of the hard work totally worth it. Each and every matter is different and it always makes me work just a little harder. The legal field is never boring!

One of the things I like least about my job are the deadlines. I am a very organized, systematic person; to have three people coming at me at once wanting something right then is very trying. It also makes me appreciate how much they value my knowledge and more specifically my legal background.

Q. What type of educational path did you pursue to become a paralegal?

A. I have worked in the legal field for 21 years, with the last 11 years as a paralegal. I began by taking courses offered by our local NALS chapter. Each month a speaker would provide legal education on a variety of subjects. I began studying for my advanced certification (known as PLS) from NALS. Once I gained that certification, I knew I needed more knowledge and education to take the next step and become certified as a paralegal. I began studying for my professional paralegal certification and passed in 2003. You can never stop learning; it is the pursuit of knowledge that drives your career path.

Q. How important is certification to career development and advancement?

A. Certification in any career shows your willingness to learn and promotes your awareness to keep your skills and knowledge current with today's trends.

Q. What are the most important professional qualities for paralegals?

A. Qualities that are most important for any paralegal are the ability to multi-task, think on your feet, and the ability to work independently. You never know how many different projects you will have to juggle, and it is that ability to prioritize your time and energy that is a must. Another important quality for a paralegal is the ability to listen. The clients will give you information, as well as the attorneys, and you need to be able to listen carefully to all of the details.

Q. What advice would you give to high school students who are interested in this career?

A. The best advice: if there is job shadowing offered, ask to work in a law firm. Ask to work with an attorney part of the time and the support staff the rest of the time. You can learn a lot by watching and get a real feel if this is the career path for you. Also, get involved in your school student council. It offers a great path to develop your leadership skills, which is a must for the legal field.

Parole Officers

QUICK FACTS

School Subjects
Government
Psychology

Personal Skills
Helping/teaching
Leadership/management

Work Environment
Primarily indoors
One location with some
travel

Minimum Education Level
Bachelor's degree

Salary Range
$28,000 to $42,500 to
$71,160+

Certification or Licensing
Voluntary

Outlook
About as fast as the average

DOT
195

GOE
04.03.01

NOC
4155

O*NET-SOC
21-1092.00

OVERVIEW

Parole is the conditional release of a prisoner who has not served out a full sentence. A long-standing practice of the U.S. justice system, parole is granted for a variety of reasons, including the "good behavior" of a prisoner, as well as overcrowding in prisons.

Prisoners on parole, or parolees, are assigned to a *parole officer* upon their release. It is the job of the parole officer to meet periodically with the parolee to ensure that the terms of the release are followed; to provide guidance and counseling; and to help the parolee find a job, housing, a therapist, or any other means of support. Parolees who break the release agreement may be returned to prison.

HISTORY

The use of parole can be traced at least as far back as the 18th century, when England, awash in the social currents of the Enlightenment and Rationalism, began to cast off its reliance on punishment by death. Retribution as the primary legal goal was challenged by the idea that reform of prisoners was not only possible but also desirable. At first, this new concern took the form of a conditional pardon from a death sentence. Instead of being executed, felons were sent away to England's foreign possessions, initially to the American colonies to fill their acute labor shortage. Although this practice actually began in the 1600s, it was not until the next century that a majority of condemned convicts were pardoned and transported across the ocean. After the American colonies gained independence in the late 18th century, England began to ship felons to Australia.

An important next step in the history of parole is the "ticket of leave," first bestowed upon transported convicts in Australia. Taking various forms, this system eventually allowed a convict to be released from government labor but only after a designated number of years and only as a result of good conduct or behavior.

In the mid-19th century, the English Penal Servitude Act abolished the practice of transporting convicts to colonies and replaced it with the sentence of imprisonment. The use of the ticket of leave, however, was kept, and prisoners with good conduct could be freed after serving a designated part of the sentence. If another crime was committed, the prisoner would be required to complete the full term of the original sentence.

Although aspects of parole were tried as early as 1817 in New York State, a complete system of conditional and early release did not emerge in the United States until the 1870s. This program, begun in New York, included a method of grading prisoners, compulsory education, and supervision by volunteers called guardians, with whom the released prisoner was required to meet periodically. By 1916, every state and the District of Columbia had established a comparable program. This system of early release from prison came to be called parole—French for word, promise, or speech—because prisoners were freed on their word, or parole, of honor.

Parole has been linked with the idea of rehabilitation since its beginning. Those on parole were given counseling and assistance in finding job training, education, and housing, but, unlike prisoners released without parole, they were also monitored. It was hoped that supervision, assistance, and the threat of being confined again would lessen the chance that released prisoners would commit another crime. Parole, however, has come to have other important functions. Prison overcrowding has commonly been solved by releasing inmates who seem least likely to return to crime. Inequities in sentencing have sometimes been corrected by granting early release to inmates with relatively long prison terms. Parole has also been used effectively as a means of disciplining disruptive prisoners while encouraging passive prisoners to good behavior. Without the incentive of parole, a prisoner would have to serve out the entire term of his or her sentence.

THE JOB

Parole officers play an important role in protecting society from crime. By helping, guiding, and supervising parolees, parole officers can reduce the chance that these individuals will again break the law and thus return to prison.

The regulations concerning parole differ from state to state. In some places, prisoners are given what are called indeterminate, or variable, sentences; if convicted of robbery, for example, an offender may be sentenced to no less than three years in prison but no more than seven. In this case, the prisoner would become eligible for parole after three years. In other places, an offender is given a definite sentence, such as seven years, but according to law may be paroled after completing a certain percentage of the sentence. Particularly heinous crimes may be excluded from the parole system.

Not all prisoners eligible for parole are released from prison. Parole is generally granted for good behavior, and those who successfully complete a drug or alcohol rehabilitation program, finish their GED (general equivalency diploma), or show other signs that they will lead a productive, crime-free life are considered good candidates for parole. In a few cases, such as prison overcrowding, prisoners might be released before they are technically eligible. The parole decision is made by a parole board or other government oversight committee.

The work of a parole officer begins when a prisoner becomes eligible for parole. A parole officer working inside the correctional institution is given the job of writing a report on the prisoner. To help determine the risks involved in releasing the prisoner, the officer's report might discuss the prisoner's family background, lifestyle before entering prison, personality, skills, and job prospects, as well as the crime for which the prisoner was incarcerated and any other crimes committed. The parole board or other oversight body reviews the report; conducts interviews with the prisoner, the prisoner's family, and others; and then decides whether the prisoner is suitable for release. In some cases, the parole officer might be called to testify or may help the prisoner prepare for the meeting with the parole board.

If released, the prisoner is assigned to another parole officer outside of the correctional institution. The initial meeting between the prisoner and this parole officer, however, may take place inside the prison, and it is there that the parole officer explains the legal conditions that the prisoner must follow. Beyond refraining from criminal activity, common conditions are attending school, performing community service, avoiding drug or alcohol abuse, not possessing a gun, and not associating with known criminals.

At this point, the parole officer tries not only to help the parolee find housing, employment, job training, or formal education, but also to provide counseling, support, and advice. The parole officer may try to help by referring the parolee to other specialists, such as a psychologist or a drug rehabilitation counselor, or to a halfway house, where the parolee can live with other former prisoners and may be assisted by drug abuse counselors, psychologists, social workers, and other professionals. Parolees with financial problems may be referred to welfare agencies or social service organizations, and the parole officer may help arrange welfare or other public assistance. This is especially important for a parolee who has a family. The parole officer also sets up periodic meetings with the parolee.

An important part of the parole officer's job may be to contact and talk with businesses that might employ former prisoners. The parole officer tries to alleviate the concerns of business leaders reluctant to hire parolees and to highlight the role of the business community in helping former prisoners begin a new life.

Much of the parole officer's work is directed toward ensuring that the parolee is upholding the release agreement. The parole officer might interview the parolee's teachers, employers, or family and might conduct other types of investigations. Records must be kept of the parolee's employment or school status, finances, personal activities, and mental health. If the parolee does not follow the release agreement, the parole officer must begin proceedings for returning the parolee to a correctional institution. In some places, the parole officer is charged with arresting a parolee who is violating the agreement.

Parole officers often have a heavy caseload, and it is not unusual for 50 to 300 parolees to be assigned to a single parole officer. With so many parolees to monitor, little time may be spent on any single case. Some parole officers are helped by *parole aides* or *parole officer trainees*. A job with similar responsibilities is the *probation officer*; some officers handle both parolees and those on probation. As the title suggests, probation officers work with offenders who are given probation, which is the conditional suspension of a prison sentence immediately after conviction. Probation is often given to first-time offenders. Like parolees, those on probation must follow strict guidelines, and failure to do so can result in incarceration. Probation officers, like parole officers, monitor the offenders; assist with finding employment, training, or education; make referrals to therapists and other specialists; help arrange public assistance; interview family, teachers, and employers; and provide advice and guidance. Those who work with children may be called *juvenile court workers*.

REQUIREMENTS

High School

If you are interested in this field, take a course load that provides adequate preparation for college studies. English, history, and the social sciences, as well as courses in civics, government, and psychology, are important subjects for high school students. Knowledge of a foreign language, particularly those spoken by larger immigrant and minority populations, will be especially helpful to a prospective parole officer. Some parole officer positions require fluency in specific foreign languages.

Postsecondary Training

The minimum educational requirement for becoming a parole officer is usually a bachelor's degree in criminal justice, criminology, corrections, social work, or a related subject. A degree in public administration, law, sociology, or psychology may also be accepted. A master's degree, as well as experience in social work or in a correctional institution, may be required for some positions.

Other Requirements

To be a successful parole officer, you should be patient, have good communications skills, and the ability to work well with and motivate other people.

EXPLORING

The best way to gain exposure to the field is to volunteer for a rehabilitation center or other social service organization. Some agencies offer internship programs for students interested in the field. It may also be helpful to call a local government agency handling parole and to arrange an information interview with a parole officer.

EMPLOYERS

Most parole officers are employed by state or county correctional departments. Other parole officers are federal employees. Probation officers generally work for the courts. Halfway houses and work release centers also hire parole and probation officers. Approximately 94,000 workers are employed as probation officers and correctional treatment specialists in the United States.

STARTING OUT

After fulfilling the necessary requirements, many enter the field by directly contacting local civil service offices or county, state, or federal parole boards. In some areas, applicants are required to take a civil service examination. Job listings are also found in the career services offices of colleges and universities and in the classified section of newspapers. Contacts leading to employment are sometimes made during

A parole officer meets with a parolee to discuss electronic monitoring.
(Bob Daemmrich, The Image Works)

internships at a rehabilitation center or other organization. Greater opportunities exist for applicants with a master's degree and for those who are willing to relocate. Many parole officers are former police and corrections officers who have gained additional training.

ADVANCEMENT

Some people enter the field as a parole officer trainee before assuming the title of parole officer. New employees are given on-the-job training to learn the specifics of their job.

There are a number of higher level positions. Beyond the job of parole officer, there are opportunities as supervisors, administrators, and department heads. Some parole officers are promoted to director of a specialized unit.

EARNINGS

The U.S. Department of Labor reports that the median annual earnings for probation officers and correctional treatment specialists (the category under which parole officers are classified) were $42,500 in 2006. Salaries ranged from less than $28,000 to $71,160 or more. Earnings vary by location and by level of government. Probation officers and correctional treatment specialists employed in state government earned a mean salary of $47,570 in 2006, while those employed in local government earned $45,380. Educational level also affects salary. Parole officers who have advanced degrees generally earn more than those with only bachelor's degrees.

Like most government workers, parole officers receive a good benefits package. Benefits include vacation days, health insurance, and a pension plan.

WORK ENVIRONMENT

Parole officers usually work out of a clean, well-lighted office in a government building, courthouse, correctional institution, or social service agency. Those who work in the field must travel to various settings, such as private homes, businesses, or schools, in order to conduct interviews and investigations.

Parole officers typically have a 40-hour workweek, although overtime, as well as evening and weekend work, may be necessary. Because of potential emergencies, some may be on call 24 hours per day, seven days a week.

The job can bring a considerable amount of stress. Many parole officers have workloads that are too heavy, sometimes approaching 300 cases at once. Frustration over not having enough time to do an effective job is a common complaint. In addition, many parolees commit new crimes despite efforts by the parole officer to provide assistance. Others may be angry or violent and thus difficult to help or counsel. The job, in fact, can be dangerous. Despite the drawbacks, many people are attracted to the field and remain in it because they want to be challenged and because they know that their work has a positive impact on public safety.

OUTLOOK

The employment outlook for parole officers is good through 2016, according to the U.S. Department of Labor. The number of prisoners has increased dramatically during the past decade, and many will become eligible for parole. Overcrowding of prisons across the United States, combined with heightening concerns over the high cost of incarceration, have prompted the early release of many convicts who will require supervision. New programs replacing prison as a method of punishment and rehabilitation are being instituted in many states, and these programs will require additional parole officers. However, public outcry over perceived leniency toward convicted criminals, particularly repeat offenders, has created demand and even legislation for stiffer penalties and the withdrawal of the possibility of parole for many crimes. This development may ultimately decrease the demand for parole officers, as more and more criminals serve their full sentences.

FOR MORE INFORMATION

For industry information, contact
American Correctional Association
206 North Washington Street, Suite 200
Alexandria, VA 22314-2528
Tel: 703-224-0000
http://www.aca.org

For information on probation and parole, contact
American Probation and Parole Association
2760 Research Park Drive
Lexington, KY 40511-8410
Tel: 859-244-8203
Email: appa@csg.org
http://www.appa-net.org

For a list of accredited bachelor's and master's degree programs in social work, contact
Council on Social Work Education
1725 Duke Street, Suite 500
Alexandria, VA 22314-3457
Tel: 703-683-8080
Email: info@cswe.org
http://www.cswe.org

For information on careers in social work, contact
National Association of Social Workers
750 First Street, NE, Suite 700
Washington, DC 20002-4241
Tel: 202-408-8600
http://www.naswdc.org

For information about the corrections industry, visit
The Corrections Connection
http://www.corrections.com

Patent Lawyers

OVERVIEW

Patent lawyers are intellectual property lawyers who specialize in securing patents for inventors from the United States Patent and Trademark Office (USPTO) and prosecuting or defending suits of patent infringements. Patent law is a blending of two fields: applied science and law.

HISTORY

The history of law dates back thousands of years, although the area of patent law is a relatively recent development. As far back as the 1300s, people sought help from lawyers and their governments to protect their ideas and inventions from theft. In the early days of the United States, there was also concern about the protection of patents and other creative endeavors. The authors of the Constitution included a provision that authorized Congress to enact a statute "to promote the progress of science and useful arts, by securing for limited times to authors and inventors the exclusive right to their respective writings and discoveries." Unfortunately, both lawyers and their clients were often frustrated in their attempts to gain support for patents and copyrights in court. By the 20th century, however, Congress and courts had begun to see innovative ideas and products as valuable to U.S. status in the global market. Today, scientists, engineers, researchers, research companies, and the citzen-inventor rely on patent law to ensure that their discoveries and advancements are protected as their property. U.S. patents protect an invention from being made, used, or sold by any party other than the patent holder for 20 years. After this time, other parties may produce, use, or sell intellectual property contained in the original patent. Patent lawyers are the unique bridge between the scientific/ technological and legal worlds, making sure their clients receive the acknowledgements for and profits from their work.

THE JOB

Individuals, groups, or businesses often seek patents for their inventions as a way to protect against others from profiting or misusing their original idea. *Patent lawyers* are attorneys that specialize in patent law, which is one branch of intellectual property law. They help clients navigate through the process of obtaining a patent from the U.S. Patent and Trademark Office. There are three different types of patents awarded in the United States depending on the subject matter. A *utility patent,* the most common, is issued to protect a process or function of an invention. *Design* patents protect the ornamental or decorative aspect of an object. *Plant* patents are issued for a newly invented or discovered asexually reproduced plant.

During the initial stage of the patent process, lawyers meet with the client to familiarize themselves with the invention. Clients describe the nature of the invention, its purpose, and how it differs from others that may already be on the market. The patent lawyer will then evaluate the technical aspect of the invention and advise the client as whether or not it is worthy of a patent. Research is often done to find similar inventions and compare technical or functional differences. A patent lawyer working on presenting a type of crayon lipstick, for example, would research all patents or patents pending for similar cosmetics, or those presented in a comparable container.

The next step in the patent process is a formal application. The lawyer drafts a detailed description of the invention, in this case the crayon lipstick. It's the lawyer's job to define what the product is and how it works. He or she may include drawings of the lipstick's holder, which show the mechanics and composition of the case, as well as composition of the actual lip color. He or she will also attach a set of claims which will define the scope of the client's rights as a patent holder. Will the patent prevent other cosmetic companies from using a holder with a similar design? Is the texture or hues of the crayon lipstick covered within the patent's boundaries?

The patent lawyer sends the completed application, additional documents, and applicable fees to the USPTO. Once received, the case is assigned to an examiner. The patent lawyer will often maintain correspondence with the examiner, provide additional information or technical drawings, or make amendments as needed to the original application. The patent lawyer will receive notification on whether or not the patent is granted. If rejected, the lawyer may file for an appeal. Once approved, a patent prevents the item or invention from being copied or sold by those other than the patent holder for a period of 20 years.

Patent lawyers may also help their clients file for patents in other countries, in case the invention is to be marketed internationally. They may also represent the client if there is evidence that the patent has been infringed.

REQUIREMENTS
High School
To prepare for this field, take college preparatory classes in high school that include the sciences (such as biology, chemistry, and physics) and government or law. In addition, take mathematics and economics classes, which will give you practice working with numbers and theories. Take history or social studies courses, which will provide you with an understanding of the development of societies, as well as the ability to turn research into a logical, progressive argument. Since much of your professional time will be spent researching documents, writing patent specifications, and presenting arguments, be sure to take English classes. These classes will help you develop your writing, speaking, and research skills. Finally, since many colleges have a foreign language requirement and patent work takes place around the world, consider adding a language to your class schedule.

Postsecondary Training
Because this is a specialized field, you will need several years of postsecondary training that include undergraduate- and graduate-level work. Like any lawyer, you will need to get a college degree before attending law school. Many aspiring patent lawyers major in physics, engineering, or the sciences (such as chemistry and biochemistry). You will also want to load up on courses as English, government, economics, and a foreign language. Patent lawyers in the greatest demand typically have Ph.D.s in a science or technology field, such as genetic engineering, chemical engineering, or biotechnology, as well as their law degree. A Ph.D. may take between four and five years of post-undergraduate coursework to complete.

Law school typically lasts three years for full-time students. As part of their entrance requirements, most law schools require potential students to take the Law School Admission Test (LSAT), which measures critical thinking and reasoning abilities. In law school you will take such classes as legal writing and research, contracts, constitutional law, and property. You should also take courses in intellectual property law, which are necessary for any type of patent lawyer. You will graduate from law school with a juris doctor (JD) degree or a bachelor of laws (LLB) degree.

Some graduates participate in credit and noncredit post-law school programs. Law schools that offer such programs include George Washington University National Law Center, John Marshall School of Law, Franklin Pierce Law Center, and New York University Law School.

Certification or Licensing

To practice any type of law, you must pass the bar exam of the state where you intend to practice. To qualify for the bar exam in most states, you must usually have a college degree as well as a law degree from a law school accredited by the American Bar Association (ABA). Many find these requirements are tough enough, but would-be patent lawyers have a much longer and harder road to travel before they can practice. First, all patent attorneys must pass another bar exam specific to patent law and given by the U.S. Patent and Trademark Office. Patent attorneys must then also prove that they have at least an undergraduate degree in one of the engineering or scientific fields that has been approved by the U.S. Patent and Trademark Office.

Other Requirements

While scientific aptitude and knowledge are clearly important for achieving success in this field, verbal skills tend to be at just as important as the more analytic, scientific ones. While just communicating with the inventor may take all your skill and scientific background, the even greater challenge often comes when you have to communicate that specialized and technical knowledge to a judge who may have no scientific or technical training.

EXPLORING

Since patent law combines the areas of science/technology and law, there are a number of ways you can explore this field. To investigate the law aspect of this career, try to get a part-time job or internship with a law office in your area. You will probably be performing tasks such as filing papers, photocopying, and answering phones, but this experience will give you an idea of what working in a law office is like. If you can't find such a job, try locating a lawyer in your area with whom you could do an information interview. Even if the lawyer is not a patent lawyer, he or she may be able to give you some insights into the practice of law and the experience of law school.

To explore the science/technology aspects of this career, consider joining a science or engineering club at your school. Ask your science or technology teacher about any contacts he or she might have with science or engineering professors at the university level. You may be able to set up an information interview with a scientist or engineer working on or having completed a Ph.D. Find out what this person likes about the field and get any advice he or she may offer to a young scientist or engineer.

EMPLOYERS

Many patent attorneys work for law firms that focus specifically on patent law or the wider field of intellectual property law (see Intellectual Property Lawyers), although some practice at firms that offer a wider range of legal specialties. Other lawyers practice at larger technology corporations that hire their own in-house counsels, or at the Patent and Trademark Office itself. For all patent lawyers, however, the work environment tends to be formal and often intense, since the amount of money at issue in patent suits is usually substantial.

STARTING OUT

Internships and clerkships are often good ways to gain experience and enter the law field. You may want to apply for a clerkship in the U.S. Court of Appeals for the Federal Court in Washington, D.C. To gain a clerkship, you should write to the judge while you are still in law school. Another option is to get a job at the U.S. Patent and Trademark Office. Finally, many people are recruited by law firms right out of law school. Your law school should have a career services office as well as offer you professional contacts through alumni that help you find a position.

ADVANCEMENT

For patent lawyers who excel at combining verbal and technical skills, advancement can be rapid and exciting. It is not uncommon for lawyers with Ph.D.s in genetic engineering, biotechnology, or other fast-growing fields to find themselves flooded with clients. The most successful of these lawyers can hope to advance to partner positions at their firms or even to establish a sufficient client base with which to start their own firms.

EARNINGS

In the law field, salaries tend to increase in predictable increments as the lawyer gains in experience and seniority. According to the U.S.

Department of Labor, the 2006 median salary for practicing lawyers was $102,470, although some senior partners earned well over $1 million a year. Ten percent earned less than $50,580. General attorneys in the federal government received $116,700 in 2006. Higher salaries are generally found in major urban areas at large firms with 75 or more lawyers.

Patent lawyers earned salaries that ranged from less than $38,999 to $120,878 or more in 2008, according to Salary.com. Fifty percent of patent attorneys earned salaries that ranged from $56,623 to $99,482.

Most lawyers receive standard benefits from their employers, including health insurance and retirement plans.

WORK ENVIRONMENT

Generally, there is a heavy workload with this career, and stress is part of the job. Successful and well-educated patent lawyers can find themselves in especially high demand, and keeping hours down to an even remotely reasonable number can be a challenge. However, even this negative aspect has its upside, since patent lawyers entering the field in the next few years should find plenty of demand for their talents. Some travel may be involved in the work, and, of course, patent lawyers must be able to work with a variety of people. In addition, these lawyers often have the benefit of having their intellectual curiosity satisfied by their work.

OUTLOOK

The U.S. Department of Labor predicts that employment for lawyers to grow about as fast as the average for all occupations through 2016, although competition for the best jobs will be intense. Patent attorneys should also have a good future. Protecting the rights of clients with new ideas and products and protecting the rights of clients who currently have patents should create many job opportunities for these specialty lawyers.

As with other law fields, the development of patent law is closely tied to the development of the industry it supports. In recent years, many biotechnology corporations, for example, have begun merging with and buying out smaller companies, resulting in fewer and larger companies. If this development continues, more companies will be large enough to hire their own in-house counsels—which will improve employment opportunities for patent lawyers who specialize in biotechnology.

FOR MORE INFORMATION

For information on all areas of law, law schools, the bar exam, and career guidance, contact
American Bar Association
321 North Clark Street
Chicago, IL 60610-4714
Tel: 800-285-2221
Email: askaba@abanet.org
http://www.abanet.org

To read the publications What Is a Patent, a Trademark and a Copyright? *and* Careers in IP Law, *visit the AIPLA's Web site.*
American Intellectual Property Law Association (AIPLA)
241 18th Street South, Suite 700
Arlington, VA 22202-3419
Tel: 703-415-0780
Email: aipla@aipla.org
http://www.aipla.org

For industry information, contact
Association of Patent Law Firms
266 Elmwood Avenue, #541
Buffalo, NY 14222-2202
Tel: 905-889-9125
Email: aplfadmin@aplf.org
http://www.aplf.org

For information about intellectual property law and degree programs, contact
Franklin Pierce Law Center
2 White Street
Concord, NH 03301-4176
Tel: 603-228-1541
Email: admissions@piercelaw.edu
http://www.fplc.edu

For information on patent law, contact
National Association of Patent Practitioners
4680-18-i Monticello Avenue
PMB 101
Williamsburg, VA 23188-8214
Tel: 800-216-9588

Email: napp@napp.org
http://www.napp.org

For information about intellectual property and job opportunities, contact the U.S. Patent and Trademark Office. Its Web site offers a link designed specifically for creative students interested in invention and includes contest information.
United States Patent and Trademark Office
Office of Public Affairs
PO Box 1450
Alexandria, VA 22313-1450
Tel: 800-786-9199
Email: usptoinfo@uspto.gov
http://www.uspto.gov

Polygraph Examiners

OVERVIEW

Polygraph examiners, sometimes known as polygraphists, use polygraph equipment and techniques to determine whether individuals have answered questions truthfully or dishonestly. Polygraphs, often called "lie detectors," are instruments that measure and record certain nonvoluntary body responses that are affected by the individual's emotional state. To judge whether the subject has answered all the questions truthfully, the examiner compares the reactions recorded for questions that are not likely to cause stress with the reactions recorded for other questions. More than 3,200 polygraph examiners are members of the American Polygraph Association.

HISTORY

Automatic body functions such as breathing and blood circulation are the basis for measuring individuals' truthfulness. There is no one physiological response that reveals a lie. However, the rates of nonvoluntary processes change in response to stress, and stress is likely to increase when an individual is lying. One of the first attempts to use this knowledge to detect deception was made in 1898, when suspected criminals were interrogated while their pulse rates and blood volumes were monitored. Tests conducted in 1914 measured the volume of the air that test subjects breathed, and tests performed in 1917 showed that changes in blood pressure also could indicate whether the subjects were telling the truth.

John A. Larson, a medical student who worked with a local police department, invented the first modern lie detector in 1921. Larson's

QUICK FACTS

School Subjects
Biology
Psychology

Personal Skills
Mechanical/manipulative
Technical/scientific

Work Environment
Primarily indoors
One location with some
  travel

Minimum Education Level
Some postsecondary training

Salary Range
$19,720 to $58,260 to
  $92,590+

Certification or Licensing
Voluntary (certification)
Required by certain states
  (licensing)

Outlook
About as fast as the average

DOT
199

GOE
02.05.02

NOC
6465

O*NET-SOC
N/A

instrument continuously recorded blood pressure, pulse rate, and respiration. His machine was called a polygraph, which means "many writings," because it recorded all these processes simultaneously. Later polygraphs incorporated galvanic skin reflex testing, which recorded the changes in the electrical conductivity of the skin resulting from changes in perspiration levels.

Polygraphs have been used in police intelligence and security investigations since 1924. Lie detector testing has sparked a great deal of controversy. Many people object to such testing as an invasion of privacy and a violation of civil liberties. The validity of polygraph tests has often been questioned, and test results are generally inadmissible in court unless the defense, prosecution, and judge agree to their use. While studies have rated the validity of polygraph examinations at 80 to 98 percent, their reliability depends on the skill and experience of the examiner.

This controversy resulted in federal legislation. In 1988, the federal government established the Employee Polygraph Protection Act, which placed strict controls on the use of polygraph testing by private employers. Businesses are prohibited from requiring polygraph testing of employees or job applicants, except for employers engaged in security services, toxic waste disposal, or controlled substances, and employers under contract with the federal government. Polygraph testing is also permitted when an individual is suspected of committing a finance-related crime.

THE JOB

Although polygraph examiners often test suspects and witnesses in criminal cases, the applications of the polygraph are not limited to police work. For example the armed forces government agencies employ polygraph examiners to screen prospective civilian employees. Private companies may also employ polygraph examiners, as well as law firms involved in civil litigation.

Before polygraph examiners meet the subject they will test, they gather information about the individual and the circumstances involved. They research the subject's childhood, medical history—including use of medications, possible emotional illnesses, or drug/alcohol abuse—and inquire if the subject has a police record. In criminal cases, they may visit the police station, the crime scene, or the morgue for information.

After gathering this information, polygraph examiners spend at least an hour with the test subject to obtain information about background, current health, and knowledge of the circumstances that led to the polygraph examination. They try to calm the subject's fears about the test by explaining how the polygraph instrument works and explaining the test procedure.

Next polygraph examiners develop test questions that are easy to understand and are not ambiguous. Before they administer the test, they read the questions to the subject to assure the subject that there will be no surprise questions. Then the examiners attach the apparatus to the individual to measure changes in certain nonvoluntary body responses.

The examiner fastens a tube around the subject's chest and abdominal area to measure the rate of the subject's respiration. A cuff similar to that found on a blood pressure meter is wrapped around the subject's arm in order to record cardiovascular activity. Two small metal plates are attached to the fingers; these record sweat gland activity. All these sensors are connected to the polygraph machine. The machine, which may consist of analog instruments or computerized polygraph instruments, records changes in the subject's breathing, heart rate, and perspiration.

The actual testing session is rather brief; a 10-question test takes about four minutes. The test may consist of control questions, which are not likely to cause stress, and key questions, which are likely to produce a strong reaction if the subject is lying. Another form of the test includes a number of similar questions, with only one question containing the correct details. Because only the guilty subject knows which question has the right details, a reaction to that question can indicate their guilt or innocence.

Some people believe they can affect their reactions by taking drugs. But a drug that reduces an individual's reactions to key questions also will reduce the individual's reactions to the control questions. Thus the test results will still show a difference between the subject's reactions when answering truthfully and when lying.

After administering the test, polygraph examiners evaluate the subject's recorded responses and then discuss the results with the individual. If it appears that the subject has been untruthful, examiners try to give individuals a chance to explain the reasons for their reactions and may even retest them later.

In addition to administering and evaluating polygraph tests, polygraph examiners keep records and make reports on test results. They may appear in court as witnesses on matters dealing with polygraph examinations, and some also teach classes in polygraph operation and interrogation techniques.

REQUIREMENTS

High School

You should take courses that help you understand how the body functions and how it is affected by stress. Courses in psychology, physiology, and biology will be especially useful. In general, take courses that will prepare you for college.

Postsecondary Training

A college major in science or criminal justice will prepare you for this career. In addition, classes in English and writing will help prepare you to write reports, and classes in public speaking will help you develop the self-confidence you will need when testifying in court.

Candidates for lie-detection schools usually need four-year college degrees, but applicants with two years of college courses in criminal investigation plus five years of investigative experience may be accepted. Polygraph training in an approved school usually takes from six to eight weeks.

You must take polygraph tests upon entering a lie-detection school to ensure you have the good moral character this field requires. During your training, you learn how to operate the polygraph, how to develop and ask questions, how to interpret polygraph charts, the legal aspects of polygraph testing, and about the physical responses the polygraph measures. You observe polygraph tests administered by others, administer the tests yourself, and hear and see recordings of your own performances. After you complete your study in lie-detection, you go on to an internship of at least six months before becoming fully qualified as a polygraph examiner.

Certification or Licensing

National standards for training—as well as the polygraph equipment used—are established by the American Polygraph Association. The American Association of Police Polygraphists offers the certified forensic law enforcement polygraph examiner designation to its members who complete educational and experience requirements.

Although approximately 29 states license polygraph examiners, licensing requirements vary. Typical requirements include a high school diploma or the equivalent, either a bachelor's degree or five years of experience as a detective, completion of polygraph training at a state-approved school, a six-month internship, and successful completion of a state-administered test.

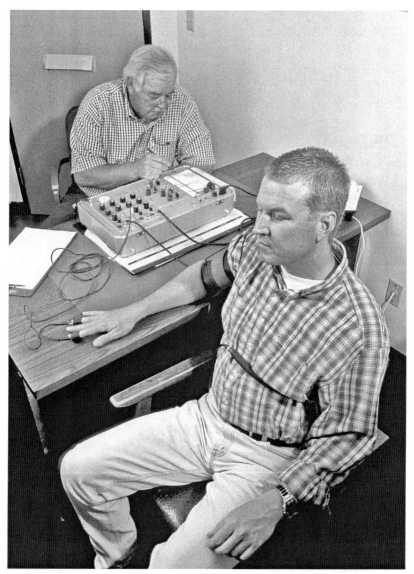

A polygraph examiner tests a subject. *(Bob Daemmrich, The Image Works)*

Other Requirements

Polygraph examiners must show good moral character and cannot have police records. You should speak and write well, be self-confident, alert, and able to maintain objectivity and self-control. You also must be comfortable working with strangers and relate well to all kinds of people. It is crucial to show fairness; you should not be influenced by such factors as economic status, race, or sex.

In addition, you must be willing to work under pressure and under a variety of conditions and should not be shocked by distressing sights. You must understand the importance of protecting your subjects' rights and maintaining confidentiality.

EXPLORING

Because polygraph examiners must obtain cooperation from their test subjects, activities that offer contact with people can provide you valuable experience. Such activities include summer work as a camp counselor and volunteer or part-time work in a hospital or nursing home. Students at some colleges can volunteer for campus security patrols to develop their observation and investigative skills.

If you live near a largely populated area, you may be able to visit lie-detection schools and talk with staff members. You also may be able to visit courts and tour police facilities. Take advantage of any opportunities you get to talk with people who conduct police or private investigations.

EMPLOYERS

Polygraph examiners are employed in many types of organizations, and their surroundings and the type of people they work with are determined by the nature of the organization. Many examiners are involved in law enforcement and may work for criminal or civil courts, police or sheriff departments, the FBI, or the Secret Service. Some work for the armed forces, and many others work for private businesses, such as retail stores, drug firms, companies that have their own security forces, and firms that provide testing services for other business organizations. The American Polygraph Association has more than 3,200 members.

STARTING OUT

Schools specializing in lie-detection often provide placement assistance for their graduates. Contacts made during internships can also provide job opportunities. Professional groups or periodicals that specialize in law enforcement and criminal justice often list job leads. In addition, qualified polygraph examiners can apply to courts and crime laboratories. Federal agencies have stricter requirements: You may need to take a civil service examination or have several years of investigative service before training in polygraph techniques.

In some cases people who are already involved in investigative work, such as police and private investigators, criminologists, and particularly military intelligence staff members, add to their skills by earning polygraph examiner certificates.

ADVANCEMENT

Polygraph examiners in civil service positions can advance through various job levels and eventually hold management jobs. Examiners who work for private security agencies can advance to such executive positions as director of operations. Polygraph examiners who are employed by business and industry in security positions may become supervisors and eventually head their department. In addition, some experienced polygraph examiners start their own agencies or work as security consultants or security systems specialists.

EARNINGS

Polygraph examiners beginning their internships may earn from $18,000 to $30,000 a year, and experienced examiners earn as much as $60,000 a year or more.

Salaries for polygraph examiners are comparable to other law enforcement investigators. According to the U.S. Department of Labor, median annual earnings of private detectives and investigators were $33,750 in 2006, with a range from less than $19,720 to more than $64,380. Median annual earnings of detectives and criminal investigators were $58,260, with salaries ranging from less than $34,480 to more than $92,590.

Examiners who are paid employees often receive such benefits as sick leave, paid vacations, medical and dental insurance, retirement plans, and bonuses.

WORK ENVIRONMENT

Most polygraph examiners work 40-hour weeks, although some work longer and irregular hours, including nights and weekends. Examiners usually work indoors, but may travel to their appointments, often carrying their polygraph equipment, which can weigh 25 pounds or more.

OUTLOOK

Because of the 1988 Employee Polygraph Protection Act restricting the use of polygraph testing, there are fewer positions for private polygraph examiners than there were before the act was passed.

However, there is increasing need for law enforcement examiners, especially in the federal government.

The growing population and increasing crime rate may create more openings for polygraph examiners in the future. Courts in at least 30 states allow the use of polygraph test results as evidence, and public pressure for reducing court backlogs may increase the use of polygraph tests.

FOR MORE INFORMATION

The following organization compiles statistics, operates a speaker's bureau, publishes a journal, offers awards to outstanding polygraphists, offers certification, provides information on approved schools, and conducts specialized education and research. For more information, contact

American Association of Police Polygraphists
PO Box 657
Waynesville, OH 45068-0657
Tel: 888-743-5479
http://www.wordnet.net/aapp

For general information on polygraph testing, as well as information on licensing and accredited polygraph schools and training, contact

American Polygraph Association
PO Box 8037
Chattanooga, TN 37414-0037
Tel: 800-272-8037
http://www.polygraph.org

For industry information, contact

National Polygraph Association
http://www.nationalpolygraph.org

INTERVIEW

Donald Imbordino is the owner of Imbordino Polygraph Examinations LLC (http://www.ImbordinoPolygraph.com) in Acworth, Georgia. He is also the president of the American Association of Police Polygraphists. Donald discussed his career with the editors of Careers in Focus: Law.

Q. Can you please tell us about your career and business?

A. Upon departing the U.S. Army as a sergeant and team chief of an atomic demolitions platoon, I joined the Addison, Illinois, Police

Department (PD). I served approximately five years in the Patrol Division and about the same amount of time in the Detective Division. I resigned from the department to accept a position as a Special Agent with the U.S. Department of Justice, Drug Enforcement Administration (DEA), Chicago Field Division. In 1987 I volunteered for the DEA's polygraph program and attended the government's polygraph school at the Department of Defense Polygraph Institute (DoDPI), Ft. McClellan, Alabama (now called the Defense Academy for Credibility Assessment located at Ft. Jackson, South Carolina).

Upon graduation from the DoDPI, I was transferred to the DEA's Atlanta Field Division Office, where I was assigned as the division's first polygraph examiner. The Atlanta Division comprises 21 offices located within Georgia, Tennessee, North Carolina, and South Carolina, and I traveled to these various locations to administer polygraph examinations when needed. Also, all DEA polygraphists are required to travel overseas to administer exams for the DEA's 77 foreign offices. I have traveled to the following countries several times: Canada, Columbia, Peru, Bolivia, Pakistan, Ghana, Thailand, Belize, Haiti, Panama, and Trinidad and Tobago.

In 1995 I was promoted and was assigned to supervise the DEA's 33 polygraph examiners until I retired at the end of 2003. This is when I established my current company, Imbordino Polygraph Examinations LLC. I now primarily work for criminal defense attorneys and administer polygraph exams to their clients to assist in their defense when the polygraph results are favorable. I have also been retained by a metro-Atlanta district attorney office and administer polygraph examinations to assist in major felony investigations. In the past 21 years I have administered approximately 3,500 polygraph examinations, and I am qualified to testify in state and federal courts as an expert witness in polygraph.

Q. Why did you decide to become a law enforcement polygraphist?

A. My first experience with the polygraph was during the application process for the Addison PD. A successful polygraph examination is required for all officers before a job offer is made. Later, when I was assigned to the Addison PD Detective Division, I utilized polygraph to assist in my investigations. It was during that time when I realized how effective polygraph was in law enforcement. Polygraph examiners resolve issues thousands of times a week in the United States, and I developed an ever-increasing interest in becoming a polygraph examiner. However, the opportunity to become an examiner did not present itself until I was employed by the DEA.

Q. What are the three most important professional qualities for law enforcement polygraphists?

A. Law enforcement experience. For a law enforcement polygraph examiner to truly be effective he or she must have first obtained several years of law enforcement experience. It is during that time when the law enforcement official learns to deal with the public and the criminal element and becomes involved in interviewing and interrogating. The best examiners I know have all brought these valuable experiences into the polygraph room. It can be quite intimidating to sit down with a serious felon and administer a polygraph. The experience and savvy one receives on the street cannot be overemphasized.

Expertise in interviewing and interrogations. It is nice when a polygraphist can tell investigators if a suspect is truthful or not, but they really display their value when they are able to obtain a confession from a deceptive examinee. One of the hardest things to do in law enforcement is to obtain a confession from a criminal who desires to maintain his or her freedom and avoid prison. Obtaining confessions is part of a law enforcement polygraph examiner's job. Therefore, each needs to become the very best interrogator possible. When a suspect is asked to submit to a polygraph exam there typically is little, if any, evidence to arrest the suspect. What the investigators really need is a confession from the guilty. I should point out that while obtaining a confession from a deceptive examinee is very rewarding, it is equally rewarding when the polygraphist is able to clear a person and remove them as a suspect.

The desire to always be professional. As in any job, there are days when we just don't feel like giving 100 percent. But a professional polygraphist must give 100 percent on each polygraph examination they administer because every examinee has something to gain and something to lose when they submit to a polygraph examination. For a criminal suspect the upside is being found not deceptive. The downside is to be found deceptive. It shouldn't matter which occurs to the polygraphist. What must matter is that the polygraphist arrives at the correct decision. This can only occur when the polygraph examination is administered at the 100 percent level of professionalism. Taking shortcuts or administering examinations outside of recognized polygraph standards of practice is almost certain to have a negative impact on the accuracy of a polygraph examination.

One of the most tiring of polygraph exams is the applicant screening polygraph. The same questions are always asked and, because of that, doing your job can easily become mundane. When I was a polygraph supervisor at the DEA, I always reminded my examiners that applicant screening is probably one of the most important jobs they have. The reason is simple: to allow someone into the DEA (or any law enforcement job) with an undetected criminal background is, at least, setting up your agency for embarrassment and, at worst, jeopardizing the safety of your fellow agents. The other side of that coin is we don't want to administer a less-than-professional polygraph causing a good candidate to be eliminated from the hiring process. I still remember how badly I wanted to become an agent, and I know each applicant wants that job just as bad. The bottom line is if a polygraphist administers each and every exam at the highest level of professionalism, errors will rarely be made.

Q. What do you like most and least about your job?
A. I like being able to assist others in determining the truth. However, I realize that this ability comes with a great amount of responsibility, so please remember what I had to say about always being professional. The part I don't like is it that it's inevitable that a very small percentage of the time a polygraphist decision can be wrong. Again, always be professional and this will be minimized. Not many things are always 100 percent accurate, but a polygraphist must still always strive for 100 percent.

Q. Can you tell us about the American Association of Police Polygraphists (AAPP)? How important is membership in a professional association to career success in the field?
A. Membership in the AAPP is restricted to law enforcement and government polygraph examiners worldwide. It is very important to belong to a national polygraph association such as the AAPP in order to obtain continuing education in the field. Each year the AAPP provides 40 hours of training in polygraph-related studies for polygraph examiners in various cities throughout the United States and produces four publications relating to the profession. It is not enough to just attend

a polygraph school. A professional polygraphist will typically attend a 40-hour training seminar every other year or more. Since becoming a polygraphist in 1987 I have attended 30 to 40 hours of continuing education every year by attending these seminars.

While employed by the DEA I was elected in 2001 as a regional director with the American Association of Police Polygraphists. I have also been elected to the positions of vice president and president, which is my current office held. Being elected as president has been one of the high points of my 21-year polygraph career.

Q. What is the future employment outlook in the field?

A. As I mentioned earlier, thousands of polygraph examinations are administered each week in the United States, and I believe the future is very promising for polygraph. Polygraph research has been an important factor in the profession—gaining scientific and legal acceptance as well as the advent of computerized polygraph systems. In its early stages polygraph surfaced just about 100 years ago, while the quest for man to know the truth has gone on for ages. Several years ago, the National Academy of Sciences conducted a study of polygraphy. It wrote in its report to Congress that while polygraph is not perfect, it is the best we have in determining truthfulness or deception when examining a single issue. Credibility assessment research has been going on in many areas in recent times, and I predict the polygraph will take on new sensors and components, making it an even better instrument of determining truth or deception in the future.

Process Servers

OVERVIEW

Process servers are licensed by the courts to serve legal papers, such as summonses, subpoenas, and court orders, to the parties involved in legal disputes. People served may include witnesses, defendants in lawsuits, or the employers of workers whose wages are being garnished by court order. Corporations can be served through their statutory agents (representatives), and unknown parties can be served as John or Jane Doe, with their true names being substituted when learned by the court. Process servers work independently or as employees of law firms and other companies.

HISTORY

Modern-day process servers owe their lineage to the English bailiff, whose powers included the serving and enforcement of common law decrees such as writs of attainder (a notice of outlawry, the loss of civil rights, or sentence of death), or habeas corpus (a call for one in custody to be brought to court). The bailiff was considered a minor court official with authority to serve the court in several ways, one of which included handling legal documents. In English literature, the most notable characterizations of bailiffs can be found in the works of the 19th-century writer Charles Dickens.

In the United States, these duties were carried out by constables until the 1930s, when the term private process server was coined to describe an official who could serve legal documents, but who had no law enforcement powers. The heavy burden of serving all the legal papers fell on the court officials and law enforcement personnel until the process server position was born. Although all criminal process service is still carried out by many sheriffs' and marshals' offices, much of the civil process service is now handled by independent process servers.

THE JOB

Process servers are responsible for assuring that people are notified in a timely and legal fashion that they are required to appear in court. Their clients may include attorneys, government agencies (such as a state's attorney general's office), or any person who files a lawsuit, seeks a divorce, or begins a legal action. As private individuals, process servers occupy a unique position in the legal system: They are court officers, but not court employees. They cannot give legal advice, or practice as attorneys.

A process server's duties are also distinct from that of the sheriff's because process servers serve papers only in civil matters, although the sheriff and constable serve in both civil and criminal matters. Criminal arrest warrants, for example, or papers ordering the seizure of property, are served exclusively by sheriffs, constables, and other law enforcement officials. To ensure that private process servers aren't mistaken for law enforcement officials, most jurisdictions forbid process servers to wear uniforms and badges or to place official-looking emblems on their vehicles.

Process servers use their knowledge of the rules of civil procedure on a daily basis as they carry out their duties. Certain types of papers—for example, a summons or court orders—expire if not served within a certain number of days. Others, such as subpoenas, must be served quickly to allow a witness time to plan or to make travel arrangements. Eviction notices and notices of trustee sales can be posted on the property in certain situations, and writs of garnishments (orders to bring property to the court) require the process server to mail papers as well as serve them.

Besides being aware of the time limits on serving a paper, process servers must know whom they are allowed to serve in a given situation. A summons, for example, can be served directly to the person named or to a resident of the household, provided they are of a suitable age. A court order or a subpoena, on the other hand, can only be served to the person named. Special circumstances also exist for serving minors, people judged to be mentally incompetent, or people who have declared bankruptcy. Many such rules and exceptions exist, and the process server is responsible for making sure that every service is valid by following these rules. An invalid service can cause excessive delays in a case, or even cause a case to be dismissed due to procedural mistakes on the part of the process server. In light of this, many process servers, or the companies they work for, are bonded and carry malpractice insurance.

A process server's job is further complicated by the fact that many people do not want to be served and go to great lengths to avoid it. Much of a process server's time is spent skip-tracing—that is, attempting to locate an address for a person who has moved or who may be avoiding service. The client may provide the process server with some information about the person, such as a last known address, a place of business, or even a photograph of the person, but occasionally process servers have to gather much of this information on their own. Questioning neighbors or coworkers is a common practice, as is using the public information provided by government offices such as the assessor's office, voter's registration, or the court clerk to locate the person. Sometimes, process servers even stake out a home or business to serve papers.

Tony Klein, from the Process Server Institute, says the clientele and the people who are served vary according to the type of work the process server does. "Some servers have clients that send primarily collection lawsuits. The defendants are generally of low to moderate income, live in low- to moderate-income neighborhoods, and might be evasive. Some servers specialize in the high end, same day, special-handling assignments involving lawsuits over substantial amounts of money."

The actual service of the paper is a simple, often anticlimactic process. The process server identifies himself or herself as an officer of the court and tells the person that he or she is being served, then hands the person the documents. If the person won't accept service, or won't confirm his or her identity, the process server will drop papers or simply leave the documents. In the eyes of the court, the person is considered served whether or not they actually touch the papers, sign for them, or even acknowledge the process server's presence.

REQUIREMENTS

High School

If process serving sounds interesting to you, get a head start now and take courses in English, political science, communication, and any law or business-related courses. Training in a foreign language can also be extremely helpful because process servers may encounter non-English speakers.

Postsecondary Training

Although college is not required, advanced courses in psychology, communication, and business would be of great benefit to a potential process server. You won't find many, if any, college or university majors called process serving. However, any college-level work in legal studies will prepare you for work in this field. The Process Server Institute (see its contact information at the end of this article) holds training seminars that focuses directly on process serving. This type of specific training will help a new process server more than the general legal studies approach.

Certification or Licensing

Any U.S. citizen who is not party to the case, is over the age of 18, and who resides in the state where the matter is to be tried may serve due process (that is, be a process server for a specific legal matter). However, people who serve papers on a regular basis usually must register with their particular state. The courts take the licensing of process servers seriously, and many jurisdictions require applicants to take a written exam; some even require an interview with the presiding judge. Alvin Esper, a process server in Indiana, recommends that all new servers obtain private detective status with their particular state: "This is not a requirement in most states or the federal courts," Esper adds, "but it can protect you when you must perform stakeouts to locate a person to be served." Because most states differ on their requirements, you should get more information from your local office of the Clerk of the Superior Court.

Other Requirements

Because process serving is a face-to-face job, people who excel in this field are usually bold, confident, and skilled at working with people. Gaining a reputation as reliable and responsible will go a long way with prospective clients who want someone who won't give up on serving papers to people. Because process servers often serve papers to people who don't want them, a certain element of danger is involved. Process servers must be willing to take that risk in some situations. Esper says, "Depending on the individual to be served, serving can be dangerous. I usually try to serve papers during daylight hours, depending on whether the neighborhood seems safe or unsafe."

EXPLORING

Check the National Association of Professional Process Servers Web site (http://www.napps.org) for process servers in your state. Contact some of these people who are working in the field now and ask for information. Speaking to attorneys, or to a local constable or sheriff's deputy, could also be helpful. Since most court records are public, you could look at actual files of court cases to familiarize yourself with the types of papers served and examine affidavits filed by process servers.

EMPLOYERS

Most process servers are independent contractors. They set up their own service business and provide process serving to individuals, lawyers, and courts. Other process servers may work for small law firms, attorney's offices, or law enforcement agencies on a full-time or part-time basis. Because courts are located throughout the country, process servers will find opportunities just about everywhere. Larger cities will have more opportunities, of course, simply due to the higher concentration of people.

STARTING OUT

Most process serving companies train their new employees and encourage them to travel with licensed process servers to familiarize them with the job. Often, the employer will assist in preparing the employee for the examination by providing them with copies of the local rules or even a study guide. Because of the flexible hours and hands-on experience with legal papers and cases, process serving is a popular job with college students, especially those who are interested in becoming attorneys themselves.

Firms specializing in attorney services will frequently train messengers and other office personnel as process servers, because they are already familiar with legal terms and documents.

You won't see many advertisements in newspapers for process servers. Instead the key to landing this job is to network with people in the legal profession. If you or someone in your family knows a lawyer, ask him or her to refer you to someone who may be interested in training a new process server.

ADVANCEMENT

A process server may start out as a legal messenger, delivering documents to law offices and filing papers with the city, state, or federal courts. In most jurisdictions, subpoenas don't need to be served by a licensed process server, so an employee of an attorney service can begin a career in process serving in this manner.

Once licensed, a process server can expect to work for a firm as either a salaried employee or a private contractor. As process servers gain experience, they typically serve more papers, and perhaps acquire bigger or more lucrative territory in which to work. In this way, advancement is also tied to the papers themselves.

In a sense, the papers that a process server delivers or serves are actually worth money, but only to the process server who delivers them. Just as private delivery companies charge for their services, process serving companies or individuals also charge for their services. The difference is that the rates are determined by the courts with the amount any given paper is worth legally fixed by law. Usually, the pricing is set in terms of the location of the delivery, the number of miles from the courthouse, and so on, but anything that makes delivery more difficult or time-consuming can add to the cost. For example, papers to be served on someone living 50 miles from the courthouse are worth more because it takes more time and money to drive 50 miles out of town. The value of those particular papers increases if they must be served within a day and the person being served has moved, forcing the process server to spend considerable time, money, and effort learning the new address. Because most process servers are independent contractors, they are rewarded for their seniority and long service with a company by being assigned to the most lucrative territories, or those areas in which the papers are worth the most.

Some process servers use the knowledge and experience they gain working for a firm to start their own businesses. Process servers who operate their own companies are responsible for all aspects of the business, from supervising and training personnel to advertising, accounting, and tax preparation.

EARNINGS

Earnings for process servers vary according to the number and type of papers served. If a process server is working as an employee of a firm, or as a private contractor, he or she can expect to earn approximately 25 to 40 percent of the total amount the firm charges the client to serve the paper. The average cost a firm charges to serve a paper is $25, but this number can vary wildly, depending on the mileage traveled to serve the paper, the number of attempts made, or any special efforts required to effect service. When taking into consideration skip-tracing, stakeout time, and other investigative efforts, the fee can be much higher.

A salaried employee who works part time as a process server can expect to make approximately $27,000, although a salaried, full-time process server can expect almost twice as much, approximately $45,000 to $50,000. The U.S. Department of Labor reports a median annual salary of $22,090 in 2006 for couriers and messengers employed in legal services. Earnings for all couriers and messengers ranged from less than $14,870 to $34,510 or more. These figures can be misleading, however. A process server can work all day and not serve any papers. The next day, he or she could make almost $600. A non-salaried process server who hustles and has a decent territory can make good money, too. "The rate depends on the type of work and the need for it," Tony Klein says. "You can make a living doing this type of work. If you work for someone, you make less than working for yourself. Every market is different; for example, in California independent servers make $2,000 to $4,000 per month."

Employees may receive such benefits as health insurance and paid vacation time.

WORK ENVIRONMENT

Being a process server requires a certain amount of hustle. The job requires that the person be part investigator, part process server, and part legal messenger. The successful process server will enjoy the more tedious aspects of sleuthing, such as tracking down routine information about someone's life.

Considering the process server's position as the bearer of bad news, it is not surprising that the job can be stressful at times. Defendants who have been avoiding service may become angry when finally served. Violence against process servers is rare but does occur. Subsequently, process servers need to remain clearheaded in stressful situations and be able to use their communication skills to their best advantage.

Process servers may work at any hour of the day in most jurisdictions, and many choose to work weekends or holidays as well. This allows for an extremely flexible work schedule, because the process server is usually the one who decides when to attempt service on a given paper. In scheduling an attempted service, the process server's main considerations are serving the paper as quickly as possible with the fewest number of attempts; if the party is not home, the process server must return later.

Many large process serving companies assign their employees fixed areas to work in, allowing a process server to become familiar with a certain section of a large city, for example, or several small towns in a given area. Even if a process server has a fixed territory, he or she can still expect to travel to a wide variety of locations. "Process serving is a lot of driving," Esper says. "Most often you are searching for the address of the person to be served." In the course of a year, a process server might serve at hospitals, prisons, schools, and any number of private offices.

When not serving papers, process servers spend much of their time working closely with attorneys, judges, and other court personnel. For this reason, many process servers dress in a professional manner. When serving, however, a process server may wear whatever he or she prefers, and many choose to dress casually. Some dress casually to appear unobtrusive, hoping that potentially evasive parties will be caught off guard, and therefore served more easily.

OUTLOOK

Employment opportunities for process servers will grow as the number of legal matters increases. The rising number of civil lawsuits bodes well for process servers, since a single case can produce anywhere from one service to dozens, when taking into account subpoenas, supporting orders, writs of garnishment, and the like.

Some sheriff's departments (long mandated by law to serve civil papers) are now beginning to rely solely on private process servers, because they cannot effectively compete with the faster and more inexpensive private process serving companies. Other jurisdictions, increasingly under pressure to justify serving civil papers at a loss, are likely to revise their laws as well.

From time to time, various jurisdictions experiment with service by registered mail, but these experiments are limited and usually not long lasting, since the most efficient way to ensure that a person has been notified is to notify him or her in person.

FOR MORE INFORMATION

To learn more about membership, contact
National Association of Professional Process Servers
PO Box 4547
Portland, OR 97208-4547
Tel: 503-222-4180
Email: administrator@napps.org
http://www.napps.org

For information about training seminars, contact
Process Server Institute
667 Folsom Street, 2nd Floor
San Francisco, CA 94107-1314
Tel: 415-495-3850
Email: psinstitute@juno.com
http://www.psinstitute.com

For a listing of current process servers, contact
United States Process Servers Association
PO Box 19767
St. Louis, MO 63144-0167
Tel: 866-367-2841
Email: info@processservers.com
http://www.usprocessservers.com

Index

Entries and page numbers in **bold** indicate major treatment of a topic.